Horses in the Air
and other poems
Jorge Guillén

Translated from the Spanish by Cola Franzen

Introduction by Willis Barnstone

CITY LIGHTS BOOKS
San Francisco

Cover design: Rex Ray
Book design: Nancy J. Peters
Typography: Harvest Graphics

Translation of this book has been assisted by a grant from the Dirección General del Libro, Archivos y Bibliotecas del Ministerio de Educación y Cultura de España.

Library of Congress Cataloging-in-Publication Data

Guillén, Jorge, 1899–
  [Poems. English & Spanish. Selections]
  Horses in the air and other poems / by Jorge Guillén : translated by Cola Franzen.
      p.   cm.
  ISBN: 0-87286-352-2 (pbk.)
  Guillén, Jorge, 1899   —Translations into English
  I. Title.
  PQ6613.05A24   1899
  861'.62—dc21   99-19321
                                                         CIP

City Lights Books are available to bookstores through our primary distributor: Subterranean Company, P. O. Box 160, 265 S. 5th St., Monroe, OR 97456. 541-847-5274. Toll-free orders 800-274-7826. FAX 541-847-6018. Our books are also available through library jobbers and regional distributors. For personal orders and catalogs, please write to City Lights Books, 261 Columbus Avenue, San Francisco CA 94133. Visit our web site: www.citylights.com

CITY LIGHTS BOOKS are edited by Lawrence Ferlinghetti and Nancy J. Peters and published at the City Lights Bookstore, 261 Columbus Avenue, San Francisco CA 94133

ACKNOWLEDGMENTS

The poems in this selection have been taken from *Cántico, Clamor,* and *Homenaje*, in the definitive edition of Guillén's work edited by Claudio Guillén and Antonio Piedra, and published by the Centro de Creación y Estudios JORGE GUILLÉN, Diputación de Valladolid, Valladolid, 1987.

Some translations presented here have appeared in the *Graham House Review*, the *Harvard Review, Delos,* and *Grand Street*.

My thanks go first of all to the family of Jorge Guillén: Teresa Guillén Gilman, Claudio Guillén, and Irene Mochi Sismondi, who have been more than generous in all ways. I owe a special debt to Teresa, who has accompanied me line by line throughout this quest; I would never have attempted it without her, and would never have been able to complete it without the constant support, advice, and expert editing of Christopher Sawyer-Lauçanno, who has carefully read every poem. Many felicitous turns of phrase are his, for which I am very grateful. Special thanks to Christopher Maurer for advice and encouragement; heartfelt appreciation to Warren Anderson, David Ferry, Frederick Fornoff, Francisca González-Arias, and the members of the translators' group of the Boston/Cambridge area, for patient listening, careful reading, and thoughtful ideas. I owe a special debt of gratitude to Nancy J. Peters and James Brook at City Lights Books, for useful suggestions and guidance, and for being true partners in this enterprise from the beginning. I have benefited from reading earlier published translations. I have not attempted to duplicate that work but for the most part have concentrated on poems not previously translated. Finally, my thanks and my love to my husband Wolfgang Franzen for his encouragement and constant support.

TABLE OF CONTENTS

INTRODUCTION

Jorge Guillén, Poet of the Secular Holy Cosmos

One lonely Sunday morning in Mexico City in 1946, Juan Delgado, a young Spaniard, said to me, "Guillermito, vamos a la corrida. Lucha Manolete." (Billy, let's go to the bullfight. Manolete's fighting.) Manolete, the grave, gentleman matador, who looked like Picasso's drawing of Quixote, was that week on all the flashy-colored posters. I don't know why—because of some passivity in a year of venture—I declined. It was not the slaughter itself, which in later years would alone have dissuaded me. In a few years Manolete, the most acclaimed figure in tauromachy, was gored in a provincial Spanish bullring near Jaén. It was December. They carried him five hours on a rocky road in an open truck to the nearest clinic. Under very primitive conditions the doctors struggled, but he died a few hours later.

Manolete and Ignacio Sánchez Mejías, the literary scholar-poet matador for whom Federico García Lorca in 1931 wrote his extraordinary elegy, *Lament for Ignacio Sánchez Mejías*, were the two fated bullfighters in the twentieth century. Manolete was the essential Spanish tragic figure, sacrificed to the ritual of an anachronistic, savage game. Sánchez Mejías was also gravely gored, and he died as a result of a series of miscalculations in the ring. Earlier, with much fanfare, he had helped to rehabilitate the baroque poet Luis de Góngora, and was a principal lecturer at the 1927 conference on Góngora in Granada, where Lorca gave his memorable lecture, "The Poetic Image of Góngora." Lorca likened the academically shunned Cordovan poet to "a leper with wounds of cold light of silver, with a fresh branch in his hands, waiting for new generations to pick up his objective heritage and his sense of metaphor." Lorca's *was* the generation of modern poets inspired and shaped by Góngora. They became known as the Generation of 1927.

Jorge Guillén was the pilot of this dynamic and diverse group.

No one then could have guessed the Generation would have such a brief life in Spain and an endless place in world literature; that at high noon a dark beast would cross the sea into Spain and savage the nation. Innocent bulls from Andalusian *fincas*, compelled into the ring, had charged and killed Manolete and Ignacio Sánchez Mejías. But when a beast of steel and fire invaded Spain nine years later under a Falange general, the sparkling Generation of 1927 darkened and was dispersed. In his terrible sonnet "Europa," Guillén evokes the cataclysm of death that was the civil war: "Again Europa and the Bull face to face."

At least there was one fantastic decade before the Bull ravaged Europa.

The year 1927 had been chosen as the group's name because it marked the three hundredth anniversary of Luis de Góngora's death. Just as American poets earlier in the century found alternate ways in the seventeenth-century English metaphysicals, the Generation of 1927 revived, invented, and made their own the surreal-fantastic Góngora with his elaborately hermetic and coldly symbolic imagery. Jorge Guillén whimsically spoke of Góngora as *el ruiseñor facilísimo del pío* (the nightingale easiest at trilling). Góngora was also a sword against sweet Spanish *modernismo* that forgot to die when vanguard movements came in. By turning to Góngora, the Generation could fully reject the esthetic mistiness of *modernista* contemporaries, whose sentimental poesy was taken from earlier French fin-de-siècle Parnassians.

The writers of the Generation of 1927 were the brightest gathering of poets in Spain since the Golden Age. Their extraordinary vitality had a counterpart in all the arts in Spain early in the century. Luis Buñuel in film, Joan Miró and Salvador Dalí in painting, Manuel de Falla, Andrés Segovia, and Pablo Casals in music. One unifying mark of the poets was their startling imagery, often surreal, based on both nature and technology. Surrealism in Aleixandre, Lorca, and Neruda was perfectly natural to the Spanish character, and unlike French automatic writing, their images were neither frivolous or indecipherable. The core group of intimates consisted of Jorge Guillén inhaling the being of mountain circumferences, Pedro Salinas whose electric princess inhabited the crystal palace of a light bulb, Federico García Lorca of a plaza of moon on the foreheads of a thousand Persian ponies, Vicente Aleixandre of fish with open eyes upholding rivers, Rafael Alberti of Cádiz with white roofs floating sailors to their morning, Luis Cernuda of squid ink gloom imprinted on patrons of pawn shops, and Miguel Hernández with oranges whose black interiors held ankles of dancing whiteness.

During the twenties and thirties, years of poetic fervor and finally civil war, exemplary Latin American poets were also living in Spain as friends and collaborators of the Generation. Jorge Luis Borges from Argentina, Pablo Neruda from Chile, César Vallejo from Peru, and Octavio Paz from Mexico. The notion of Spain and Latin America as one vibrant poetic entity has an analogue in Golden Age poetry in Spain whose last great voice was that of Sor Juana Inés de la Cruz, the seventeenth-century Mexican nun.

The spell of literary rebirth of the '27 Generation persisted until July 18th of 1936. On that day Generalísimo Francisco Franco, with the military backing of Fascist Italy and Nazi Germany, invaded Spain with Moroccan troops and plunged the nation into three years of civil war. The catastrophic war was followed by a rabidly repressive dictatorship whose order persisted until the general's death in the winter of 1975. Death and exile dissipated poetry in Spain. Lorca fell before a firing squad in a field outside Granada in 1936. In the same year Miguel de Unamuno died in his sleep under house arrest soon after he had denounced Franco's generals at a meeting at the University of Salamanca, where he was the rector. Spain's older major poet, Antonio Machado, died on February 22, 1939 in the French border town of Collioure, having crossed into France just a step ahead of the victorious Nationalist armies. Miguel Hernández, the youngest of the great poets of the Generation, was imprisoned, sentenced to death, a term later commuted to thirty years. The self-taught goatherd, master of Spanish prosody, wrote his poems of light and death in his cell as four centuries earlier the mystical poet Saint John of the Cross, confined to his prison cell in the Carmelite monastery in Toledo, composed his dark night of the soul. Hernández was not yet thirty-two when in 1942 he died of tuberculosis and misery in the Torrijos prison hospital. Vicente Aleixandre, bed-ridden for seven years, could not leave Madrid. He alone remained as a voice of dissent and futurity for younger poets.

For others of the Generation there was exile. Alberti went to Argentina, Cernuda to Mexico, Juan Ramón Jiménez stayed in Puerto Rico, Pedro Salinas and Jorge Guillén came to the United States. There was one upside. In their diaspora, the poets composed. Guillén, living and teaching at Wellesley College in the United States from 1938 to 1957, completed and published in Buenos Aires in 1950 *Cántico*, his huge book of books, which he had begun thirty-one years earlier when he was an instructor in Spanish at the Sorbonne.

After Spain succumbed to European Fascism (the Falangists imported the Fascist salute and gave their newspaper the name *La Facha*), hundreds of thousands fled, from every class and age, fearing imprisonment and the epidemic of executions. Spanish villages sprang up in southwestern France, and there were such communities all over western Europe and the Americas. Mexico, which never recognized the Franco regime, was a primary host nation to the Spanish exiles. Among its specific gestures to the Republican cause, Mexico invited five hundred Spanish war orphans to be housed in their country. In Mexico City in 1946 and 1947 when I was a student at the National Autonomous University, I lived in a small room on the roof of an orphanage, and there began my formal connection with Spaniards of the war diaspora.

When, at nineteen, I left Mexico and went to the summer language schools at Middlebury College in Vermont, I met Luis Cernuda and Jorge Guillén, who was visiting Pedro Salinas, then a lecturer in the Spanish Language School. Thereafter, I saw and corresponded with Don Jorge regularly for thirty-five years. There were family meals in Cambridge, meetings and readings in Boston, conversations in our apartments in New Haven, at Yale, and Indiana. Our last talk was in Málaga, Spain, in 1982, where the poet had gone to live after Franco died. When I published a translation of Pedro Salinas's *La voz a ti debida (My Voice Because of You),* Guillén wrote its splendid introduction. I was lucky to have known him.

Jorge Guillén was born in Valladolid on January 18, 1893, and educated in Madrid and Switzerland. In 1913 he took a Master's degree at the University of Granada. He was in Paris as a lecturer in Spanish at the Sorbonne from 1917 to 1923. In 1924 Guillén took his doctorate at the University of Madrid, and thereafter taught at the universities of Murcia, Oxford, and Seville. Finally, in 1938, in mid-civil war, he came to Wellesley College where he remained until his retirement.

In Paris, in 1921, he married Germaine Cahen, who died in 1947. Fourteen years after her death, he married Irene Mochi Sismondi in Bogotà. When I noted one evening in Cambridge at his daughter Teresa's house that Guillén was wearing two wedding rings, he said with enjoyment and candor for all to hear that he had never taken the first ring off, and when he remarried he added a new ring to his finger. He would not take that ring off either. Guillén was a man incapable of pettiness. He applied his creative standards of austere beauty and rigor to his own work, never judgmentally to others. One of his colleagues once told me with wonder, Jorge Guillén was the only person in the academy who never spoke ill of anyone. However, I do remember clear, sorrowfully sharp words when he spoke of Franco, whose officers had executed his friend Lorca. Guillén was the Aguilar editor of Lorca's complete works and letters. Jorge Guillén died back in his Spain in 1984.

In his vast and intricately perfect five-hundred page book *Cántico (Canticle),* 1928–1950, Jorge Guillén celebrated the ecstasy of breath, the oblivion of being, the existence of things, the space of horses grazing the meadow of the sky. He is a poet of felicity. But in his next book, *Clamor,* 1957–1964, he was musically and surreally dark, acknowledging the earth's dissonance and the balance of an alien nether land. In *Clamor* he joins light to darkness. Finally, in his third volume, *Homenaje (Homage),* 1967, Guillén wrote an homage to the world and its voices of memory.

There are poets who write one book, which is their bible. Charles Baudelaire's *Fleurs du Mal,* Whitman's *Leaves of Grass,* Emily Dickinson's unpublished fasciles, Guillén's *Cántico.* These committed poets spend their lives tinkering with and expanding their bible. To make his canticle into a full bible, Guillén added layer after layer—tercets, quatrains, *décimas* (ten-liners), sonnets, and free verse to edition after edition—until in the thirty-first year of its composition, he brought *Cántico* to a stop. Its subtitle *fe de vida*, means "faith in life," but the phrase is also a bureaucratic term for identity card. His long canticle was his faith in life and his ordinary identity. With the appearance of *Clamor* and *Homage*, however, he no longer had a single bible that he was expanding and perfecting. Then Guillén slyly housed his three books of poetry in a new volume, creating a single trinity under one title: *Aire Nuestro (Our Air)*, 1957. So the poet of absolutes and warm perfections, of dizzy spaces of poetry that map the cosmos, was back once again with his single bible. *Our Air*.

Jorge Guillén is a poet of spacial and temporal essences, which he delineates in his passionately smart poems. His exultation is his sudden and surprising vision of things. Everything stands in a luminous circle around his being. He is the poet of affirmation, of the great *sí*, which like Rilke's touchable distances, he finds everywhere. Guillén is a pantheist, but in a form essentially opposed to a romantic view. Unlike the romantics, who see the world as a mirror of themselves, Guillén, by contrast, sees man and woman as a fragmentary mirror reflecting the world. He does not endow the world with existence to enhance himself in its reflection. On the contrary, the pre-existent world endows him with being. It does not depend on him. He depends on it. His being is from the world.

> O perfection! I depend
> On the total beyond,
> I depend on things!
> Without me they are and become!

The poet's metaphysical passion is for reality—but not necessarily the visible landscapes of a Leopardi or Wordsworth. "Reality, not realism," Guillén states. He is attracted by the essences of the visual world, an abstraction of it, which is at once more intense and permanent. He is the geometer of modernity, observing the surfaces of the earth and the spheres as well as the exact circles and squares of the underlying structures, with the result that his mode of perception makes the poem a form of literary cubism.

The external world will not, however, impinge on the poet's being without an act of will by the poet. Things in the external world, like molecular particles, have a tension and hidden movement, and, whether man or woman or nature, are taut with desire to touch and be one with each other. Until the will acts, however, the poet feels pain, famine, and thirst. Guillén speaks of a torrid desolation, a shadowy sidewalk that shudders with hidden bulls as they crash head on. Fulfillment comes when his "cold dream becomes a love which is water." His thirst is slaked when he drinks in the abstraction of eternity.

> Ah, bringing revelation,
> the water of an ecstasy
> Upon my thirst slakes
> Eternity—Drink!
>
> *(translated by W. S. Merwin)*

As a poet of absolutes, seeking to express fundamental laws of being and nature, Guillén has returned to the earliest physicists in the West, the Presocratic philosophers, who were concerned with describing the elementary particles that underlie all matter. These philosopher-scientists called them, as we do, atoms, that which cannot be cut, the indivisible. How did they express themselves? Normally, in poetry or poetic axioms. It is curious that the most scientifically oriented philosophers before the twentieth century resorted to poetry as a means of expressing truth. Though many philosophers wrote poetically—Nietzsche, Bergson, Santayana, even Plato—only the earliest Greek atomists, or Latin imitators such as Lucretius, used formal verse to express philosophy. Guillén is with the Presocratics who sought the indivisible that connected the underlying invisible matter. Like them, he has one central notion: we are. The *we* includes himself, you, me, things, the world. The creative surprise occurs in waking to an awareness of being. Striving to make real the forces between himself and everything around him, he says, "I am not Narcissus," and affirms, "There is no solitude. There is light between everyone. I am yours. Light, nothing more." The theorem in his poems might read: Light is in me. The same light is in you, in things, in the world. We, with the same light in us, are one. We move from "we are" to "we are *one*." To capture in words the living world, Guillén invented an original poetic speech, the language of precise ecstasy. At this point he is edging toward the secular mystic. The cosmos is his domain.

Jorge Guillén is concerned with the underlying essence of the cosmos, an essence, he discovers, that is the same outside and within him. So there is a double wakening. He not only wakes, with the force of the ferocious sun trampling him, to his own being, but to existence elsewhere. His connection to that ring outside is love. To express all this, he invents a language of passionate abstractions that he designates as visual objects. Before him, only Emily Dickinson had the specific craft and intuition to make the abstract an object that could fall down a hill or rise in her like a thought.

Is there a larger pattern to Guillén's absolute rigor as he explores the labyrinths of consciousness with a goal of union with the other? There is.

While he is opposed to the translation of his experience into any creed or religious purpose, he has in his steps to metaphysical union found the way and the experience of the mystics. But can a secular writer, one I've called kin to physicists, be considered a mystic? He is a godless mystic. To understand the term, I turn to the mystical poet Saint John of the Cross (San Juan de la Cruz), the Spanish poet he most resembles and from whom he derived the title of his grand work, *Cántico*. The basis for the modern poet's secular mysticism is the apparent loss of self, the union, and the ecstasy of human love.

The major authority for speaking of John of the Cross's poetry as secular is Guillén himself. To my knowledge, he is the one critic who distinguishes between the religious mystical process of Saint John's devout trance and the luminous earthly creations in the poems themselves, which are a love of sensuality, tenderness, and oblivion. Guillén rejects Saint John the religious mystic within his poetry—as opposed to Saint John the religious mystic in his life experiences or in his commentaries. In his formal mysticism, the Doctor of Nothingness (*el Doctor de la Nada*) appears to follow Philo of Alexandria's ladders that rise from darkness to illumination and union, his *via negativa, via iluminativa,* and *via unitiva.* But even in his "Dark Night of the Soul Poem," Saint John uses what he claims is the only simile for union with God, which is the fusion of lovers. If we read what the poems say, rather than what he and others say they say, his poems celebrate the love of the full woman and man. As such, he is the first Spanish poet of the Golden Age to bring the body fully into poetry, to depart from the Platonic idealizations of Dante and Petrarch that dominate Renaissance love poetry throughout Europe. In Saint John's attempt to escape world and body, he brings world and body into magnificent focus. Guillén perfectly understood this paradox of sensuality and mystical rapture in Saint John. In describing it he gives a succinct description of his own credo:

> San Juan's extraordinary adventure, his fusion with the Absolute, leads him to write, in the most relative and concrete manner, poems of human love—some of the most beautiful the world has known. . . . For his inner life gives rise to the most lofty affirmation of the world and its creatures . . . San Juan del la Cruz achieves a poetry that is everything: illumination and perfection.

In these notions of affirmation of the world and its creations and poetry that is "illumination and perfection," we find elements of secular mysticism equally in John of the Cross and Guillén. Both follow the mystic's path psychically, if not theologically, from darkness into light and union—John by practice, if not intention; Guillén by clear intention and practice. The latter's movement from small to larger being, from self to ecstasy, is translated not into religious speech but into the workings of passion and intellect. He is consumed, forever on a trip to earthly ecstasy as his soul becomes body, and that fusion is an explosion of being:

> (The soul returns to the body,
> Aims at the eyes
> And collides,) Light! It invades
> My entire being. Wonder!

No poet, with the possible exception of Saint John, has lived so fully and affirmatively in the felicity of that orgasmic union of his being, the lover in this world, now, on this planet, in the geometric firmament of our universe.

Cola Franzen has translated Jorge Guillén. That fact is a celebration. Without inflation, without fear, she has chosen Guillén's chaste lexicon of perfection. She does not falter. Guillén has been translated in the past by many of America's finest poets, W.S. Merwin, Mark Strand, Richard Wilbur, Richard Howard, and Barbara Howes, among others. And they have translated Guillén amazingly well, a poet who should, like Emily Dickinson, be impossible to translate. But the impossible is the only worthwhile text to translate, the one with character that not only survives but thrives in translation. I would say that only Elizabeth Bishop in her translations from Portuguese and Spanish has the absolute certainty that we read in Franzen's versions of Guillén, where each line appears fresh and at the same time reborn in English. Many write about translation (I am one of the abusers), and many judge those who practice the art of poetic re-creation. In the instance of Cola Franzen's work, it is enough to read and forget that hers is not the original. In giving us such splendid versions, she fulfills Octavio Paz's axiom that an original text is a translation and a good translation is an original text.

Willis Barnstone

PRIMAVERA DELGADA

Cuando el espacio sin perfil resume
    Con una nube
Su vasta indecisión a la deriva,
    —¿Dónde la orilla?—
Mientras el río con el rumbo en curva
    Se perpetúa
Buscando sesgo a sesgo, dibujante,
    Su desenlace,
Mientras el agua duramente verde
    Niega sus peces
Bajo el profundo equívoco reflejo
    De un aire trémulo . . .
Cuando conduce la mañana, lentas,
    Sus alamedas
Gracias a las estelas vibradoras
    Entre las frondas,
A favor del avance sinuoso
    Que pone en coro
La ondulación suavísima del cielo
    Sobre su viento
Con el curso tan ágil de las pompas,
    Que agudas bogan . . .
¡Primavera delgada entre los remos
    De los barqueros!

SLIVER OF SPRING

When space without contour concludes
    in a cloud,
its vast indecision gone adrift,
    —Where the shore?—
while the river's curving course
    goes on
seeking in twists and turns, sketching
    its outcome,
while the hard green water
    disavows its fish
beneath the deep ambiguous reflection
    of a tremulous breeze . . .
when morning guides its slow
    row of poplars
thanks to the rhythmic wakes
    among the fronds,
aided by the sinuous onrush
    that synchronizes
the smooth undulation of the sky
    above its wind
with the swift swish of the bubbles
    briskly rowing . . .
Sliver of spring between the oars
    of the boatmen!

UNA VENTANA

El cielo sueña nubes para el mundo real
Con elemento amante de la luz y el espacio.
Se desparraman hoy dunas de un arrecife,
Arenales con ondas marinas que son nieves.
Tantos cruces de azar, por ornato caprichos,
Están ahí de bulto con una irresistible
Realidad sonriente. Yo resido en las márgenes
De una profundidad de trasparencia en bloque.
El aire está ciñendo, mostrando, realzando
Las hojas en la rama, las ramas en el tronco,
Los muros, los aleros, las esquinas, los postes:
Serenidad en evidencia de la tarde,
Que exige una visión tranquila de ventana.
Se acoge el pormenor a todo su contorno:
Guijarros, esa valla, más lejos un alambre.
Cada minuto acierta con su propia aureola,.
¿O es la figuración que sueña este cristal?
Soy como mi ventana. Me maravilla el aire.
¡Hermosura tan límpida ya de tan entendida,
Entre el sol y la mente! Hay palabras muy tersas,
Y yo quiero saber como el aire de Junio.
La inquietud de algún álamo forma brisa visible,
En círculo de paz se me cierra la tarde,
Y un cielo bien alzado se ajusta a mi horizonte.

A WINDOW

The sky dreams clouds for the real world
with matter enamored of light and space.
Today dunes scatter over a reef,
sands with marine waves that are snows.
So many chance crossings, by fanciful caprice,
there in plain view with an irresistible
smiling reality. I dwell on the edges
of solid transparent depths.
The air is enclosing, displaying, enhancing
the leaves on the branch, the branches on the trunk,
walls, eaves, corners, pillars:
Calm proof of the evening,
requiring a window's tranquil vision.
Details chime with their surroundings:
smooth pebbles, there a fence, then a wire.
Every minute finds its own aureole,
or is it fancy dreaming this glass?
I am like my window. I marvel at the air.
Beauty so limpid, now so in accord,
between the sun and the mind! There are polished words,
but I would like to know as the June air knows.
The poplar's stirring makes a visible breeze,
in a circle of peace the evening encloses me,
and a soaring sky adapts to my horizon.

ARROYO CLARO

El arroyo
Se rinde a su destino: lo más bello es muy poco.

Trasparencia.
Por el arroyo claro va la hermosura eterna.

No, no hay ninfas.
La claridad es quien descubre la delicia.

Clara el agua
A los ojos propone profundidad de fábula.

Y unos peces,
De súbito relámpagos, soñándose aparecen.

CLEAR STREAM

The stream
yields to its destiny: the loveliest is very little.

Transparency.
Along the clear stream goes eternal beauty.

No, there are no nymphs.
Clarity is the one who discovers delight.

Clear water
suggests to the eyes the fable's depths.

Now a few fish,
sudden lightning, dream themselves into view.

CABALLOS EN EL AIRE

(Cinematógrafo)

Caballos.
Lentísimos partiendo y ya en el aire,
¿Van a volar tal vez?

La atmósfera se agrisa.
¡Cuánto más resistente
Su espesura más gris!
Con lentitud y precaución de tacto
Las patas se despliegan
Avanzando a través
De una tarde de luna.
Muy firme la cabeza pero sorda,
Más y más retraída a su silencio,
Las crines siempre inmóviles
Y muy tendido el lomo,
Los caballos ascienden.
¿Vuelan tal vez sin un temblor de ala
Por un aire de luna?
Y sin contacto con la tierra torpe,
Las patas a compás
—¿Dentro de qué armonía?—
Se ciernen celestiales,
A fuerza de abandono misteriosas.
¿O a fuerza de cuidado?

Inútiles, se entregan los jinetes
—¿Para qué ya las bridas?—
A las monturas suaves y sonámbulas,
Que a una atracción de oscuridad cediendo

HORSES IN THE AIR

(Motion picture)

Horses.
Slowly slowly lifting into the air,
will they fly perhaps?

The atmosphere becomes gray,
How much more solid now
the denser gray!
Slowly and with cautious touch
the legs unfold
advancing across
an evening sky with moon.
Unswerving the heads, noiseless,
more and more withdrawn into silence,
the manes still motionless
backs outstretched,
the horses ascend.
Will they fly perhaps with no tremor of wing
at the moon's pace?
And without touching the clumsy earth
the feet keeping time
—to what music?—
hover celestial
by virtue of mysterious abandon.
Or by virtue of caution?

No longer needed, the riders yield
—what use are bridles now?—
to the smooth sonambulant steeds.
Lured by darkness, they

Se inclinan otra vez hacia la tierra,
Sólo por fin rozada
Sin romper el prodigio,
Rebotando, volando a la amplitud
Sin cesar fascinante.

Avanzan y no miran los caballos.
Y un caballo tropieza.
¡Con qué sinuosidad de cortesía
Roza, cae, se dobla,
Se doblega a lo oscuro
Se tiende en su silencio!
Hay más blanco en los ojos.
Más aceradamente se difunden
Los grises
Sobre el inmóvil estupor del mundo.
Las manchas de gentío
Se borran
Tras vallados penosos
Con su oscura torpeza de rumores.
Los caballos ascienden, bajan, pisan,
Pisan un punto, parten,
A ciegas tan certeros,
Más sordos cada vez, flotantes, leves,
Pasando, resbalando.
¡Qué ajuste sideral
De grises,
Qué tino de fantasmas
Para llegar a ser
Autómatas de cielo,
Espíritus—estrellas en su trance
Seguro sin premura!

lean again toward the earth,
barely grazing it at last
without breaking the wonder,
rebounding, flying off to the endlessly
fascinating expanse.

The horses move onward not looking.
And one stumbles.
With supreme sinuous courtesy
it touches, falls, curls,
curves toward the dark,
races on immersed in silence!
The eyes show more white.
The steelier grays
disperse
over the motionless torpor of the world.
Behind woeful barricades
blotches of crowds
with their crude dark murmurs
fade away.
The horses ascend, descend, tread,
tread on a point, move on,
blindly with utter accuracy,
more and more quietly, floating, light,
passing, slipping.
How skillfully the sidereal grays
mesh,
how artfully the phantoms
become
automatons of the sky,
spirits—stars in their trance
unhurried, secure!

¿Sin premura de fondo?
Esta pasión de lentitud ahora
¿No es todavía rápida,
No fué ya rapidez?
Rapidez en segundos manifiesta:
Visibles y tangibles,
Desmenuzan el vértigo
De antes
En aquel interior de torbellino:
Corpúsculos, segundos, arenisca
De la más lenta realidad compacta.

¡Gracia de este recóndito sosiego!
El animal se cierne,
Espíritu por fin,
Sobre praderas fáciles.
¡Allá abajo el obstáculo
Sobre el suelo de sombra!
Silencio. Los rumores del gentío
Por entre las cornisas y las ramas
Desaparecerán,
Callarán los insectos entre hierbas
Enormes,
Y follajes de hierro
Se habrán forjado a solas.
Alguna flor allí
Revelará sus pétalos en grande

¡Qué lentitud en ser!
Corred, corred, caballos.
Implacable, finísima,
La calma permanece.
¡Cuántas fieles ayudas primorosas
A espaldas de la prisa!

Unhurried entirely?
That passion for slowness now,
is it not yet quick?
was it not already quickness?
Quickness in obvious seconds,
visible and tangible,
that stop the gyrations
of before
in that center of the whirlwind:
Corpuscles, seconds, sandstone
of the slowest compact reality.

Grace of such cherished tranquillity!
Spirit at last,
the animals hover
over gentle meadows.
There below the obstacle
over the dark earth.
Silence. Murmurs of the crowd
from cornices and branches
will disappear.
In the spacious grasslands insects
will hush,
and iron foliage
will have forged itself alone.
Some flower there
will unfurl its petals to the full.

How slow in becoming!
Gallop, horses, gallop.
Implacable, elegant,
the calm endures.
So many unfailing exquisite props
behind haste!

Envolviendo en su gris
Discurre la paciencia
Por entre los corpúsculos del orbe,
Y con su red se extiende
Sobre las lentas zonas resguardadas.
Entre una muchedumbre de segundos
Se ocultan, aparecen
Los cuerpos estelares
—Y esos caballos solos—
Arriba solos sobre el panorama.
¡Cascos apenas, leves y pulidos
Pedruscos!

Entre los cielos van
Caballos estelares.
¿Caballos?

Enfolding in its gray,
patience roams
among the corpuscles of the sphere,
extends its net
over the slow sheltered zones.
Among numberless seconds
they hide, then reappear,
the stellar bodies
—and those horses alone—
above alone over the panorama.
Hint of hooves, light and polished
pieces of stone!

Soaring through the skies
go stellar horses.
Horses?

EL DESTERRADO

Corroborating forever the triumph of things.
—Walt Whitman

La atmósfera, la atmósfera se deshilacha.
Invisible en su hebra desvalida,
A sí mismo el objeto se desmiente.
Ronda una mansedumbre con agobio de racha.
Todo es vago. La luna no puede estar ausente.
Así, tan escondida,
¿Eres tú, luna, quien todo lo borra o lo tacha?
Torpe, quizá borracha,
Mal te acuerdas de nuestra vida.

El mundo cabe en un olvido.

Esta oscura humedad tangible huele a puente
Con pretil muy sufrido
Para cavilaciones de suicida.

Cero hay siempre, central. ¡En este plaza
Tanta calle se anula y desenlaza!

Y de pronto,
            ¡paso!
                    Con suavidad cruelmente
Discreta
Va deslizándose la pérfida bicicleta.
Pérfida a impulso de tanto perfil,
¿Hacia qué meta
Sutil
Se precipita
Sin ruido?
Lo inminente palpita.

16

THE EXILE

The atmosphere, the very atmosphere unravels.
Invisible in its graceless fiber
the object disavows even itself.
The gentle air prowls bent by squalls.
Everything is nebulous. The moon cannot be missing.
This way, so hidden,
is it you, moon, erasing and blurring everything?
Clumsy, drunk perhaps,
remembering so little of our lives.

The world fits into our forgetting.

This dark tangible dankness smells of bridge
with well-worn stone railing
for mock musings about suicide.

Zero is always there, central. In this plaza
so many streets are cancelled out and undone

And suddenly
          Out of the way!
                    Smooth ruthless
discreet
a treacherous bicycle whizzes past.
Treacherous momentum of pure profile
rushing toward
what subtle
goal
without making a sound?
The impending moment throbs.

¿El mundo cabe en un olvido?

Y entre dos vahos
De un fondo, nube ahora que se agrieta
Con una insinuación de cielo derruido,
La bicicleta
Se escurre y se derrumba por un caos
Todavía modesto.

—¿Qué es esto?
¿Tal vez el Caos?
           —Oh,
La niebla nada más, la boba niebla,
El No
Sin demonio, la tardía tiniebla
Que jamás anonada.
Es tarde ya para soñar la Nada.—

Devuélveme, tiniebla, devuélme lo mío:
Las santas cosas, el volumen con su rocío.

The world fits into our forgetting?

Between two breaths
from below, a cloud now splits
showing a hint of ravaged sky.
The bicycle
slips past and plummets into a chaos
modest still.

"What is this?
Chaos, perhaps?"
                              "Oh,
the fog, nothing more, the silly fog.
The *No*
with no demon, the dallying darkness
that never destroyed anything.
It's late now to dream up *Nothing*."

Give me back, darkness, give me back what's mine:
the blessed things, their bulk and their dew.

VIVIENDO

La ciudad se dirige hacia las brumas
Que son nuestro horizonte en los suburbios
Plomizos, humeantes bajo nubes
Que el sol poniente alarga desgarradas
Por colores apenas violentos,
Verdoso violado enrojecido.
Engrandece el crepúsculo.

Amable, la avenida
Nos expone planeta humanizado,
Nos arroja tesoros a los ojos,
Nos sume en apogeos.
Y los ruidos se juntan, se atenúan:
Murmurada amalgama
Pendiente.

Irrumpe una estridencia.
Atroz motor minúsculo trepida.
. . .Y otra vez se reanuda el vago coro,
Favorecido por la media voz
De calles
A cielos abocadas.

Bajo los rojos últimos
En grises, verdes, malvas diluidos,
Siento mías las luces
Que la ciudad comienza a proyectarme.
Mucha imaginación lo envuelve todo,
Y esta máquina enorme bien nos alza,
Inseparable ya de nuestras horas

LIVING

The city moves toward the fog,
our horizon in the suburbs,
leaden, steaming, beneath clouds
lengthened by the setting sun, torn
by slightly violent colors,
verdant violet reddened.
The twilight expands.

The friendly avenue
shows us a more human planet,
hurls treasures at our eyes,
immerses us in summits.
And the noises converge, subside:
Murmured amalgam
pending.

Strident outburst.
Dreadful little motor vibrates.
. . . And once again the vague chorus resumes,
favored by the low tone
of streets
open to the skies.

Beneath the last reds
in grays, greens, thin mauves,
I feel the lights the city
projects toward me are mine.
Much imagination envelops everything,
and that enormous machine lifts us high,
inseparable now from our days

Y de nuestros destinos.
Gran avenida—donde estoy—fulgura.

Todo avanza brillando,
Tictac
De instante sobre instante.
Con él yo me deslizo,
Gozo, pierdo. ¿Me pierdo?

Ternura, de repente, por sorpresa
Me invade.
Una ternura funde en una sola
Sombra del corazón
La ciudad, mi paseo.
Me conmueve, directa revelándose,
Común sabiduría. . .
Moriré en un minuto sin escándalo,
Al orden más correcto sometido,
Mientras circula todo por sus órbitas,
Raíles, avenidas.
Sin saberse fugaces,
Los coches
Me escoltan con sus prisas,
Me empujan,
Y sin querer me iré
Desde estos cotidianos
Enredos
—Entre asperezas y benevolencias—
Hasta ese corte que con todo acaba.
¡Telón! Un desenlace no implicado
Quizá por la aventura precedente:
Afán, quehacer, conflicto no resuelto.

Pero ya la cabeza

and our destinies.
The grand avenue—where I am—glitters.

Everything advances shining,
ticktock
instant after instant.
I let myself go with it,
rejoice, get lost. Lose myself?

Tenderness suddenly, surprisingly,
invades me.
Into one shadow of the heart
a tenderness fuses
the city, my stroll.
Common wisdom, suddenly surfacing,
moves me . . .
I will die some moment without fuss,
subject to the most correct order,
while everything keeps to its orbit,
rails, avenues.
Not knowing they are fleeting,
the cars
escort me, rush me,
urge me along,
and not meaning to I will leave
these daily
entanglements
—some harsh some sweet—
until that cut that ends it all.
Curtain! An outcome not implied
perhaps by the earlier adventure:
work, longing, unresolved conflict.

But now the mind

De sienes reflexivas
Reconoce la lógica
Más triste.
Voy lejos. Me resigno. Yo no sé. . .
Y el tránsito final
—Sobre un rumor de ruedas—ya me duele.

Está el día en la noche
Con latido de tráfico.
El cielo, más remoto, va esfumándose.
Esa terraza de café, más íntima,
Infunde su concordia al aire libre.

Cruzo por un vivir
Que por ser tan mortal ahincadamente
Se me abraza a mi cuerpo,
A esta respiración en que se aúnan
Mi espíritu y el mundo.

Mundo cruel y crimen,
Guerra, lo informe y falso, disparates. . .
No importa.
Impuro y todo unido,
Apenas divisible,
Me retiene el vivir: soy criatura.
Acepto
Mi condición humana.
Merced a beneficios sobrehumanos
En ella me acomodo.
El mundo es más que el hombre.

Así voy por caminos y por calles,
Tal vez
Errando entre dos nadas,

in its own reflections
recognizes the saddest
logic.
I will go far away. I am resigned. I don't know . . .
And the final passage
—over a drone of wheels—already pains me.

The day is present in the night
pulsing with traffic.
The sky, more remote, vanishes.
This café terrace, more intimate,
suffuses the outdoors with its harmony.

I traverse a way of living
so mortal that it clings
to my body, this breath where
my spirit and the world intertwine.

Cruel criminal world,
war, amorphous and false, nonsense . . .
No matter.
Impure and all intermingled,
hardly divisible,
living holds me: I am creature.
I accept
my human condition,
make myself at home
thanks to superhuman favors.
The world is more than man.

Thus I travel roads and streets
perhaps
wandering between two nothings,

Vagabundo interpuesto.

Me lleva la avenida
Con esta multitud en que se agrupan
El pregón, el anuncio, la persona,
Quiebros de luces, roces de palabras:
Caudal de una ansiedad.
Por ella
Logro mi ser terrestre,
Aéreo,
Pasaje entre dos nubes,
Conciencia de relámpago.

interjected vagabond.

The avenue carries me along
with this multitude in which cluster
shouts, sirens, announcements, people,
swerves of light, swishes of words:
stream of anxiety
through which
I attain my earthly being,
volatile,
passage between two clouds,
alert to lightning.

LUCIÉRNAGA

La noche aleja el prado,
Gris azul en lo negro. De pronto fulge un punto
Verde muy amarillo aligerado
Por tan rápida huida
Que apenas es ya vida
Cuando se desvanece, se enluta hacia un presunto
Casi aniquilamiento.

Desde la sombra mía yo presiento
La hermosura—que es luz—de aquel instante
Breve, feliz, mortal: relámpago de amante.

FIREFLY

Night displaces the meadow,
gray blue on black. Sudden flare
of a bright yellow-green point made pale
by such quick flight
that it is now barely life
when it vanishes, darkens toward
a seeming near extinction.
From my shadow I sense
the beauty—which is light—of that instant
brief, happy, mortal: lover's lightning flash.

INVASIÓN

Quiero dormir y me inclino
Sin moverme hacia lo oscuro.
Pero el magín es camino
Que traspasa todo muro.

Subiendo está el sol naciente.
Oigo el trote de un caballo.
Despiertan ojos de puente.
No quiero buscar y hallo.

El caballo se me ha ido
Por su vía, tan ajena.
No escucho. Me roza el ruido
Que la luz desencadena.

Sueño, reposo, fatiga.
Caballo, coche, campana.
Vivir no es soñar. Que diga
Si yo finjo mi ventana.

Ya el caballo es pensamiento.
En mí trota y trota fuera.
La ventana da el aliento
De una invasión verdadera.

INVASION

I want to sleep and lean over
without moving toward the darkness.
But the mind is a path
that pierces every wall.

The infant sun is rising.
I hear the trot of a horse.
Spans of a bridge open.
Not wanting to seek I find.

The horse has left me
going its way, so alien.
I don't listen. The noise unleashed
by the light grazes me.

Sleep, rest, toil.
Horse, car, bell.
Living is not dreaming. What if
I invent my window.

Now the horse is thought.
It trots inside me and trots outside.
The window gives a breath
of a real invasion.

BAR DE ESQUINA

Se comprime el bar en la esquina
De unas calles muy populosas,
Y el gran estrépito del tráfico
Da velocidad a la hora,
Que en el bar—son las dos, las tres—
Corre tanto que no se nota:
Ocios, negocios, hasta luego,
Carreras de caballos, hola . . .
Y con gracia la vida va,
Mortal, inagotable, corta.

CORNER BAR

The bar on the corner wedged
between two very crowded streets,
and the deafening din of traffic
speeds up the hour
that in the bar—it's two, three—
runs so fast no one notices:
pastimes, business, see you later,
news from the race track, hello . . .
and life slips smoothly past,
mortal, persistent, short.

LOS SUPREMOS

Ha dejado de llover
Torrencialmente. La plaza
Resuena con su domingo
Sonoro entre muchas caras,
Bajo los grandes laureles
Prietos ya de su algazara
Crepuscular. ¡Qué de pájaros
Dominando a todos cantan,
Últimos conquistadores,
Ay, Cortés, de Cuernavaca!

THE SUPREME ONES

The torrential rain
has stopped. The plaza's
noisy Sunday ricochets
among the many faces gathered
beneath the tall laurels
laden with crepuscular
commotion. So many birds
chattering, dominating everybody,
latest conquistadors,
O, Cortez, of Cuernavaca!

POTENCIA DE PÉREZ

I

Hay ya tantos cadáveres
Sepultos o insepultos,
Casi vivientes en concentraciones
Mortales,
Hay tanto encarcelado y humillado
Bajo amontonamientos de injusticia,
Hay tanta patria reformada en tumba
Que puede proclamarse
La paz.
Culminó la Cruzada. ¡Viva el Jefe!

El Jefe, solo al fin,
Cierra la puerta, siente alivio.
                  Solo,
Sin el peso de un mundo abominable,
Sin la canalla que le adora y teme,
Que le adora y detesta.
Es él quien todos alzan para todos,
Y en ellos estribado,
Se aúpa,
Adalid de su Dios.
La victoria es santísima.

¡Sí! Se columbra junto al Jefe a Dios,
Tan propicio a la causa.
Una común empresa los reúne.

¿Cómo entender que un hombre, sólo un hombre
Doblegue a tantos bárbaros unidos

POWER OF PEREZ

I

There are now so many cadavers
buried or unburied,
barely alive in moribund
concentrations,
so many imprisoned and humiliated
beneath mountains of injustice,
so much transformed country entombed
that they can proclaim
peace.
Culmination of the Crusade. Long Live the Leader!

The Leader, alone at last,
closes the door, feels relieved.
                                        Alone,
without the weight of a hateful world,
without the rabble that adores and fears him,
adores and detests him.
Elevated by all for all,
leaning on them
he whoops himself up,
Champion of his God.
The victory is most holy.

Yes! By the Leader's side is God,
so auspicious to the cause.
A common undertaking joins them.

How to comprehend that a man, only a man,
could force so many barbarians together

En vientos
De acosos homicidas,
O en grupos de cabezas más agudas
Que ese cerebro acorde a tal fajín?

Fajín hay de Cruzado fulgurante,
Ungido por la Gracia
Del Señor, que es el guía.

Guía a través de guerra
Tan cruelmente justa
Para lanzar un pueblo a su destino.

Destino tan insigne
Que excluye a muchedumbres de adversarios
Presos o bajo tierra:
No votan, no perturban. ¡Patria unánime!

Sobreviven los puros,
De tan puros cubiertos
En el gran sacrificio
Por las sangres malvadas.

Oh Jefe, nunca solo: Dios te encubre.

II

Refulge un orden nuevo
Que se inscribe en mayúsculas: el ORDEN.

La Verdad se desposa con el Régimen,
Está infusa en el Jefe,
Desciende a las cabezas elegidas,

into the gales
of homicidal pursuits,
or compel sharper minds
than his to agree on that General's sash?

Sash of the resplendent Crusader,
anointed by the Grace
of the Lord, who is the guide.

Guide by means of war
so cruelly just
as to plunge a people to its destiny.

Destiny so illustrious
that it eliminates hosts of adversaries
imprisoned or beneath the earth:
they don't vote, they don't disturb. Unanimous country!

The pure survive,
so very pure as to be covered
by wicked blood
in the great sacrifice.

O Leader, never alone: God harbors you.

    II

A new order shines forth
written in capital letters: ORDER.

Truth is wedded to the Regime,
bestowed on the Leader,
anoints the chosen heads,

Es lujo de uniformes,
Dirige los fusiles:
Donde ponen la bala está el error.
Apunten fuego.

¡Fuego!

Cuanto más resplandece la Verdad,
Más difuntos la cantan.
Ni un asomo de duda ya se enfrenta
Con esta profusión de condenados.
Donde hay Fe santamente se asesina.
El Jefe
No, nunca se equivoca.

Al revólver del puro no le falla un disparo,
Y la Verdad avanza destruyendo
Por entre tantos brazos y muñecas,
Por entre tantos puños,
Vellosos hacia el sol.

¡Júbilo de camisas! Pueblo sano:
Erige el porvenir, la edad de oro,
Azul de estío azul
Sobre ese laberinto de oficinas,
De negocio entre muros
De una implacable desnudez abstracta.
¿Corruptelas? No importan.
Importa sólo la total justicia.

Y la justicia invade.
Sonríen en talleres buenos mozos.
Cara al trigo ondeado por la brisa
Ríen, ríen doncellas laboriosas.

is luxury of uniforms,
guides the guns:
wherever the bullet strikes it finds a fault.
Aim fire.

     Fire!

The more Truth glitters
the more corpses sing it.
Not a hint of doubt now confronts
that profusion of wretches.
With Faith they assassinate in saintly fashion.
The Leader,
never ever makes a mistake.

The revolver of the pure does not miss a shot,
and the Truth advances ravaging
among so many arms and wrists,
so many hairy fists,
reaching toward the sun.

Jubilee of shirts! Healthy people:
they are building the future, the golden age,
blue summery sky-blue
over that labyrinth of offices,
of deals struck between walls
of an implacable abstract nakedness.
Corrupt them? No matter.
All that matters is total justice.

And justice invades.
Handsome lads smile in workshops.
Faces to the wheat waving in the breeze
toiling girls keep on laughing.

¿Disidente? Ninguno
Que no sea culpable.
Diferir es manchar la gran blancura
De la Historia aclarada.
¿Y el pensamiento bajo su silencio?
Preferible el disfraz.
Mentid.

Mentid y levantad los brazos,
Los brazos o sus puños,
Y las lenguas. Cantad con energía,
Cantad.
El país es el coro de los coros.

III

CORO DE BUROCRACIA

La ley levanta
Frente al oficial cacumen
La sacrosanta
Letra que todos consumen.

No se interprete la Letra.
Su cuerpo mismo es sagrado.
Si una mente la penetra,
Se nos desploma el Estado.

Requisitos y papeles,
Eso es lo bueno,
Con sus colas de peleles,
Pies en el cieno.

Dissident? Not one
who's not guilty.
To differ is to stain the great whiteness
of a clarified History.
And the thought behind the silence?
Disguise is preferable.
Lie.

Lie and raise your arms,
your arms or your fists,
and your tongues. Sing out with vigor,
sing.
The country is a chorus of choruses.

III

CHORUS OF BUREAUCRACY

The law raises high
before official acumen
the most sanctified
Letter for all to consume.

No one explains the Letter.
Its very body is godly.
If a mind should ever pierce it,
the State would surely topple.

Lots of forms and paperwork,
that's what brings us luck,
with their long lines of jerks,
feet mired in the muck.

Cuando un jefe toca un timbre,
Algo nuevo se enmaraña.
Nadie rehuya la urdimbre
De nuestra araña sin maña.

Vale candor
Si alguna vez se estremece
—¡Señor, Señor!
—que pase el número trece.

IV

CORO DE POLICÍA

Correctos, brutales,
Sutiles, entramos,
Salimos, rivales
De lobos y gamos.

Por nuestras pistolas
Ilustres bergantes
Que viven de trolas
Son más elegantes.

Repertorio fino:
Engaño, tortura,
Muerte en el camino
Más que cárcel dura.

Tal es nuestra dicha
Que hasta el más honesto
Desde alguna ficha
Cae en nuestro cesto.

When the boss touches a bell,
more snarls—inner to outer.
No one escapes the roiled pell-mell
of our blundering spinning spider.

Frankness often works
if sometimes it quakes.
—Señor, Señor!
Number thirteen is next.

IV

Correct and brutal,
scheming we come
and we go, rivals
of hyenas and wolves.

By means of our pistols
illustrious hooligans
who live from false libel
now parade like elegants.

Our refined repertoire
Deception and torture,
death in the street
instead of harsh prison.

Such is our fortune
that even the most honest
thanks to some document
will land in our basket.

El Jefe ya sabe
Que es Primer Cruzado
Mientras sea suave
La guarda a su lado.

V

Tan elocuente suena la verdad
Que al universo guía
Con la voz de figuras invisibles,
De figuras parlantes:
Onda en retorno de propagaciones.

¡Estribillo, supremo!

No habrá jamás vocablo
Sin poderío de fascinación
Si la sentencia es falsa, ronda y zumba,
Se va, reaparece
Con ese dulce ahínco de los sueños
Durante la vigilia,
Y el curso de las horas
Más apaciblemente naturales
Serpea
Bajo el sol y la luna.

Y todo se relaja.

El hombre es bueno: cree, cree, cree.
Vocablo tan mascado es realidad
Tangible.
Hombres buenos: creed, creed, creed.

The Leader well knows
he's First Crusader
while tame patrols
stand at his shoulder.

V

So eloquent sounds the truth
guiding the universe
with the voice of invisible figures,
talking figures:
Surging waves of disseminations.

Refrain, supreme!

Never will there be word
without power to captivate,
even false sentences prowl and hiss,
go, reappear
as urgently as sweet dreams
during half-sleep
and in the course of the most
peaceful natural hours,
slither along
beneath the sun and the moon.

And all grows calm.

Man is good: he believes, believes, believes.
Word so chewed over is tangible
reality.
Good men: believe, believe, believe.

Y todo se relaja, cede, cae.

¿La impostura es cemento?
¿O el material más fuerte del gran Orden
Va por el aire de la primavera,
Ya música
De los más fabulosos disparates?

No hay más verdad que la vociferada
Por tantos pregoneros
Que miran al oriente de un fajín
Augusto.

¿Aquel semblante escucha?
Un pensamiento al fin sin pensamiento
Corona
La siesta de una oreja adormecida.
¿Qué verdad clausurada no adormece?
No, no difiera nadie.
Y mejor si difiere. Que se humille.
¡Punto en boca! Vencida:
Que todo se deforme
Roído
Por encima de muertos y de presos
Y desterrados, todos enterrados.

Canten aún los coros.

VI

CORO DEL PARTIDO

Somos los únicos amos
Del presente y del futuro.

And all grows calm, yields, falls.

The fraud is made of cement?
Or does the strongest material of the great Order
go through the spring air,
now music
of the most fabulous ravings?

No other truth than the clamor
raised by the horde of proclaimers
who look to the dawning of a grandiose
sash.

That countenance listens?
A thought at last without thought
crowns
the siesta of a drowsing ear.
What cloistered truth does not slumber?
No, no one disagrees.
Better if someone does disagree. Let him grovel.
Zip the lip! Vanquished:
Let everything be deformed
corroded
on top of the dead, the prisoners,
and the exiles, all buried.

The choruses keep singing.

VI

CHORUS OF THE PARTY

We are the only masters
of the present and the future.

49

Sin desfallecer lanzamos
La pelota contra el muro.

No hay libertad, trasto viejo.
Poder encumbra al Partido.
Muera el infeliz conejo
Que vaga a solas huido.

Pensamos todos a una
Sobre un desierto compacto
Para que a todos reúna
Como emblema el puro cacto.

Bien acariciada empresa
De largo alcance y botín
Es montura que no cesa
De ofrecernos brida y crin.

Sin desfallecer lanzamos
La pelota contra el muro.
Somos los únicos amos
Del presente y del futuro.

VII

CORO DE CLERECÍA

Humildes, reverentes,
Graves de dos en dos,
Conducimos las gentes
        A Dios.

Recto poder profano,
Si a Dios no desafía,

50

Never pausing we keep bouncing
the same old ball against the wall.

No more freedom, old and ragged.
It's power exalts the Party.
Death to the luckless rabbit
on the run alone unguarded.

We all think as one
over a solid desert
so all may gather as one
under our emblem, a cactus.

Highly cherished venture
of wide scope and booty,
mount always ready,
with bridle, saddle, spurs.

Never pausing we keep bouncing
the same old ball against the wall.
We are the only masters
of the present and the future.

VII

CHORUS OF THE CLERGY

Humble, reverent,
solemn, by twos and threes,
we guide the people
        to God.

Righteous profane power,
if it doesn't rival God,

Besa el anillo en mano
Del guía.

Dios gana nuestras luchas,
Y aunque se llame Alá,
En todas nuestras huchas
Está.

La nación nos reserva
Su profundo gobierno,
Sin Dios caterva sierva
De infierno.

Las llamas al hereje
Le hacen señas: ven, ven.
Dios es con Nos el eje,
Amén.

VIII

Y los coros preparan el desfile.

Es fiesta.
El día redondea un sol muy rico
De plumajes, charoles, armas nítidas.
A tanta pompa en rigidez aplaca,
Ya resplandor, el triunfo así arrojado
Brillantemente a todos.

(Menos a los caídos
Bajo tierra o en tierra de una ausencia
Forzosa o escogida.)

kisses the ring on the hand
        of the guide.

God wins our battles,
although his name be Allah,
and in all of our coffers
        he's there.

The nation destines for us
its firmest control:
without God, the mob is servant
        of hell.

Flames beckon
to the heretic: Come, come.
God is with Us the fulcrum,
        Amen.

VIII

And the choruses prepare the parade.

Festivities.
The day complete with lavish sun,
plumes, shiny leather, spotless arms.
Such stern pomp, now splendor,
appeases, the gleaming triumph
thus flung down to all.

(Except to the fallen
beneath this soil, or on another, absent
by force or choice.)

Distante, muy distante,
La multitud entre rumores calla.
Lejos contempla al Jefe en su tablado,
Solo sobre su escena,
Solo entre sus insignias y sus cruces,
Que el aislamiento ahondan,
Jerárquico,
Hasta una soledad
Profunda,
Bajo aquel sol—tan cómplice—
Definitiva glorificación.

¡Tirano!

Las tribunas, repletas,
Yerguen sus cortesías.
(No quieren saber más: vigor, victoria.)
Pájaros y follajes inocentes
Participan de patria y regocijo.

Los soldados, islotes uno a uno,
Por masas dirigidas
Concurren a un compás
Que mueve un solo cuerpo
De muchas piernas y de muchos brazos
Unánimes, anónimos:
Máquina entre las máquinas mortíferas
Que anuncian
Con sus dóciles brillos
La espera de una guerra.

Todo funciona como si la sangre
También corriese por el artefacto
Que desfila, total:
Ajeno a casi todos.

Distant, very distant,
the crowd's murmurs cease.
Far away the Leader on his platform,
alone above the scene,
alone among his insignias and his crosses,
deepening his isolation,
hierarchical,
reaching a profound
solitude,
beneath that sun—so complicitous—
final glorification.

Tyrant!

The reviewing stands, full,
display their courtesy signs.
(All they wish to know: vigor, victory.)
Birds and innocent foliage
part of fatherland and rejoicing.

The soldiers, each an island,
directed by masses
agree on a rhythm
that moves a single body
of many legs and many arms
inanimate, anonymous:
a machine among deadly machines
proclaiming
with their obedient glitter
anticipation of a war.

Everything works as if blood
were also running through the contrivance
parading past, complete:
detached from almost everyone.

Y los fríos columbran a los fríos,
Y pasan
Los a compás también espectadores.

Un dos, ficción, un dos, ficción, un dos.

IX

La ficción se disipa en soledades.
A solas silencioso el tan nombrado
No queda ni ante sí,
Figura sin figura
Si no se la proponen los espejos.
Ni el esplendor antiguo del palacio
Donde reside ahora y se repliega,
Ya rey,
Puede impedir que el hombre verdadero
Se insinúe en la pausa,
Y aparezca ese Pérez vergonzante
Que embrollo y perifollo casi ocultan:
Un Pérez, ay, terriblemente Pérez,
El más terrible Pérez, que se llama
Pérez y que lo es.

Ahí,
Céntrico ahí, perdura.
¡Cuántos le necesitan y le inventan!
Que mande
Sosteniendo aquel Orden: su desorden,
Sus bandos,
Sus chanchullos patrióticos.
La tiranía avanza
Con excluyente fuerza

But cold faces discern the cold,
and passing by
those keeping step spectators also.

One two, untrue, one two, untrue, one two.

IX

The untrue evaporates into loneliness.
Alone, silent, the one so often named
is invisible even to himself,
figure without figure,
unless mirrors suggest one to him.
Neither the ancient splendor of the palace
where he now resides and to which he now withdraws,
already king,
can prevent the true man
from wheedling his way into the pause,
and then appears that shameful Pérez
that fraud and frippery almost hide:
A Pérez, oh, so terribly Pérez,
The most terrible Pérez whose name is
Pérez and that's what he is.

There,
centermost, he endures.
How many need him and fabricate him!
Let him command
upholding that Order: his disorder,
his edicts,
his patriotic swindles.
The tyranny goes on
with power to wipe out

Sobre miles y miles de caídos
Por ley de asesinato,
Entre las muchedumbres
De boca amordazada.
Dogma, sangre, dinero.
Y Pérez, Pérez, Pérez.

Ensangrentado Pérez bien ungido,
Tan dueño del presente,
Un presente muy largo sin futuro
De historia que no aboque a la catástrofe.
Todos la temen, nadie la desea:
Que el tirano persista.

Y el tirano conduce,
Cruel, solemnemente a ciegas listo,
Sin cesar infalible,
Su artilugio triunfal
A su quebrantamiento más penoso,
Más vano:
Explosión en el choque
—Y todos ya lo auguran—
Contra el vacío mismo. No hay futuro.
Se adivina latente
Clamor con un furor
Que llenará de espanto
La escena de la farsa:
Muertos y muertos, muertos.

thousands and thousands of fallen
by the law of assassination,
among the throngs
of gagged mouths.
Dogma, blood, money.
And Pérez, Pérez, Pérez.

Bloodied Pérez well anointed,
absolute master of the present,
a long, long present with no future
that does not lead to catastrophe.
Everybody fears it, nobody wants it:
Let the tyrant persist.

And the tyrant,
cruel, solemnly blindly ready,
forever infallible,
drives his triumphal contraption
to its most painful, emptiest
breaking point:
explosive shock
—that everyone now foresees—
against emptiness itself. There is no future.
Yet barely divined a latent
clamor, with a furor
that will strike this farcical
scene with terror:
the dead, the dead, the dead, the dead.

See Translator's notes, p. 239.

ALBA DEL CANSADO

Un día más. Y cansancio.
O peor, vejez.
            Tan viejo
Soy que yo, yo vi pintar
En las paredes y el techo
De la cueva de Altamira.
No hay duda, bien lo recuerdo.
¿Cuántos años he vivido?
No lo sabe ni mi espejo.
¡Si sólo fuese en mi rostro
Donde me trabaja el viento!
A cada sol más se ahondan
Hacia el alma desde el cuerpo
Los minutos de un cansancio
Que yo como siglos cuento.
Temprano me desperté.
Aun bajo la luz, el peso
De las últimas miserias
Oprime.
            ¡No! No me entrego.
Despacio despunta el alba
Con fatiga en su entrecejo
Y levantándose, débil,
Se tiende hacia mi desvelo:
Esta confusa desgana
Que desemboca a un desierto
Donde la extensión de arena
No es más que cansancio lento
Con una monotonía
De tiempo inmerso en mi tiempo,

THE WEARY MAN'S DAWN

Another day. And weariness.
Worse, old age.
                    So old
am I, I saw the walls
and roofs of the caves of Altamira
being painted.
No doubt about it, I remember it very well.
How many years have I lived?
Not even my mirror knows.
If it were only my face
that the wind had worked over!
With every sunrise the weary minutes
as long to me as centuries
bore ever deeper
from the body into the soul.
I awoke early.
Even in the light, the weight
of the latest miseries
bears down.
                    No! I do not surrender.
Slowly dawn appears,
fatigue knitting the brow
and rising feebly,
bends toward my wakefulness:
This confusing reluctance
that leads to an expanse of sand
is nothing but slow weariness
monotonous time
immersed in my time,
the one I drag along, the one dragging me,

El que yo arrastro y me arrastra,
El que en mis huesos padezco.
Verdad que abruma el embrollo
De los necios y soberbios,
Allá abajo removidos
Por el mal, allá misterio,
Sólo tal vez errabundos
Torpes sobre sus senderos
Extraviados entre pliegues
De repliegues, y tan lejos
Que atrás me dejan profunda
Vejez.
     ¡No! No la merezco.
Día que empieza sin brío,
Alba con grises de enero,
Cansancio como vejez
Que me centuplica el tedio,
Tedio ¿final? Me remuerde
La conciencia, me avergüenzo.
Los prodigios de este mundo
Siguen en pie, siempre nuevos,
Y por fortuna a vivir
Me obligan también.
          Acepto.

the one I suffer from in my bones.
Certainly the muddle
there below is crushing:
the foolish and haughty
moved by evil or mystery,
occasional clumsy
wanderers on their path
straying among folds
of more folds, so far away
they leave behind for me
the depths of
old age.
       No! I do not deserve it.
A day that begins with no verve,
dawns with January grays,
and weariness like old age
that quintuples my boredom,
final boredom? My conscience
gnaws at me, shames me.
The wonders of this world
are still in place, always new,
and as luck would have it, they bid
me live also.
       I accept.

HOTEL DE AMBOS MUNDOS

¿No se interrumpe la vida?
Dentro
De mi cabeza dormida
Frente a una función me encuentro.

Un teatro
Consigue imponerme a mí
Sus invenciones. Ahí
Nunca dos y dos son cuatro.

¿Eres, orbe tan absurdo,
Mi creación y me alteras?
¿Tales imágenes urdo,
Y me oprimen verdaderas?

Sufro, desespero, lloro,
Se me ahoga la garganta.
Alguien canta
Porque perdí mi tesoro.

Pero esta función es corta.
Me despierto,
Y el cambio no me conforta.
¿Cuál lo cierto?

HOTEL OF BOTH WORLDS

Does life not pause?
Inside
my sleeping head
I find myself before a performance.

A theater
succeeds in imposing its inventions
on me. There
two and two are never four.

Are you, absurd sphere,
my creation and yet you transmute me?
Do I weave such images
that truly oppress me?

I suffer, despair, weep,
my throat chokes up.
Someone is singing
because I have lost my treasure.

But this performance is short.
I awake.
And the change does not console me.
Which is real?

See Translator's notes, p.242.

LA SANGRE AL RÍO

I

Lucha, lucha civil,
Una lucha lastrada
Por algo más profundo,
Más noble que la
Y bajo la difícil paz yacía,
Y con tanta presión que en una tarde,
Una tarde de sábado . . .

Sabemos lo ocurrido.

No valdría la pena
Contar su historia a quien jamás la olvida.
El lúgubre recuerdo
Se resiste a salir
De su ya perezosa
—Tan doliente el meollo—somnolencia.
Tal dolor, sin embargo, busca el aire.

Silencio. La memoria
No duerme bien. Insomne, con ahínco
Nocturno,
Exige claridad,
Habla acaso a la luna.

II

Llegó la sangre al río.
Todos los ríos eran una sangre,
Y por las carreteras

BLOOD IN THE RIVER

I

Struggle, civil struggle,
a crushing struggle
for something deeper,
nobler than peace,
and beneath the difficult peace lay,
so heavily weighted that one evening,
a Saturday evening . . .

We know what happened.

It would not be worthwhile
to tell his story to someone who never forgets it.
The grievous recollection
resists emerging
from its still sluggish
somnolence—so painful the marrow.
And yet such pain seeks open air.

Silence. The memory
sleeps fitfully. Wakeful,
with nocturnal zeal,
it demands clarity,
speaks perhaps to the moon.

II

The blood reached the river.
All rivers were one blood,
and along the roads

De soleado polvo
—O de luna olivácea—
Corría en río sangre ya fangosa,
Y en las alcantarillas invisibles
El sangriento caudal era humillado
Por las heces de todos.

Entre las sangres todos siempre juntos,
Juntos formaban una red de miedo.
También demacra el miedo al que asesina,
Y el aterrado rostro palidece,
Frente a la cal de la pared postrera,
Como el semblante de quien es tan puro
Que mata.

Encrespándose en viento el crimen sopla.
Lo sienten las espigas de los trigos,
Lo barruntan los pájaros,
No deja respirar al transeúnte
Ni al todavía oculto,
No hay pecho que no ahogue:
Blanco posible de posible bala.

Innúmeros, los muertos.

Crujen triunfantes odios
De los aún, aún supervivientes.
A través de las llamas
Se ven fulgir quimeras,
Y hacia un mortal vacío
Clamando van dolores tras dolores.

Convencidos, solemnes si son jueces
Según terror con cara de justicia,
En baraúnda de misión y crimen

of sun-drenched dust
—or of olive-colored moon—
blood now muddy ran in the river,
and in the unseen sewers
the bloody flow was disgraced
by everybody's excrement.

In the mingled bloods everybody together forever,
together they wove a net of fear.
Fear blights the murderers as well;
just as the terrified face pales
before the lime of the final wall,
so does the countenance of the one so pure
that he kills.

Coiled into wind, the crime whistles.
The sprigs of grain feel it,
the birds surmise it,
it lets no passerby breathe
nor those still in hiding;
no breast left unstifled.
possible target of possible bullet.

Numberless, the dead.

Triumphant hatreds crackle
from those who still, still survive.
Glimpsed through the flames
the glitter of chimeras;
toward the deadly void,
wailing, go sorrows upon sorrows.

In a tumult of mission and crime
zealots, grave-faced if judges
colluding with terror with semblance of justice,

Se arrojan muchos a la gran hoguera
Que aviva con tal saña el mismo viento,
Y arde por fin el viento bajo un humo
Sin sentido quizá para las nubes.
¿Sin sentido? Jamás.

No es absurdo jamás horror tan grave.
Por entre los vaivenes de sucesos
—Abnegados, sublimes, tenebrosos,
Feroces—
La crisis vocifera su palabra
De mentira o verdad,
Y su ruta va abriéndose la Historia,
Allí mayor, hacia el futuro ignoto,
Que aguardan la esperanza, la conciencia
De tantas, tantas vidas.

III

Sobre los intereses, las pasiones,
Por entre conciliábulos y cálculos
Luce una idea frente al combatiente.
Hasta el más criminal se justifica,
Ante sí mismo a solas,
Con razón que se explaya en el silencio,
Más hondo
Que el guirigay lanzado
Por voces y altavoces.

¿Quién no se juzga justo,
Quién no se siente justo hasta la muerte,
Su propia muerte o la del enemigo,
Impulsado también por la justicia,
Una justicia inmensa entre cadáveres?

thrust multitudes into the great bonfire
whose intense fury stokes the very wind,
and at last the wind burns beneath a smoke
meaningless perhaps for the clouds.
Meaningless? Never.

Such grievous horror is never absurd.
Among the shifting events
—self-sacrificing, noble, sinister,
ferocious—
the crisis shouts its word,
lie or truth,
and History opens its path,
broader there, toward an unknown future,
awaited by hope, heedful
of so many, many lives.

III

Above interests and passions,
among conspiracies, calculations,
an idea gleams before the combatant.
Even the greatest criminal justifies himself
to himself alone
with arguments that flourish in silence,
deeper
than the gibberish hurled
by shouts and loudspeakers.

Who would not judge himself just,
who would not feel himself just until death,
his own death or the enemy's,
driven also by justice,
the enormous justice offered by dead bodies?

Terrible Buena Fe contradictoria,
Errabunda con farsas y con odios,
Los odios más opacos.
Por encima, radiante,
La Causa.

Doble Causa en conflicto irreductible,
Doble faz de este Jano que se muere,
Y jadea, jadea.

¿Jadea todavía?

Y por entre los muertos,
El todavía vivo va orientándose.
Se esclarecen los rumbos.
Mudas peroraciones y retóricas,
El vivir verdadero
Conduce a la razón por su camino.

La verdad se abre paso día a día,
Entre el agua y la sed,
Entre el pan y las hambres,
Por entre el viento libre y soleado,
O sobre rejas, muros y cerrojos.

Pese a tantos engaños, ¿qué es visible?

Bajo un sol no oficial,
Que no es de nadie cómplice,
Manchas, oscuras manchas
Extiende la miseria sobre muchos
Entre los viejos y los nuevos prósperos.

Terrible contradictory Good Faith,
roving with mask and hatred,
the most benighted hatred.
Above, resplendent,
The Cause.

Double Cause in never to be resolved conflict,
double face of that dying Janus
who gasps and gasps.

Gasping still?

And in the midst of the dead,
those still living slowly get their bearings.
The course of events becomes clearer.
Soundless harangues and rhetoric,
true living
leads reason along its path.

Day by day truth makes its way,
between water and thirst,
bread and hunger,
free and sunny breezes,
or over railings, walls, past latches.

Despite so much deceit, what is clear?

Beneath a non-official sun,
nobody's accomplice,
spots, dark spots
spread misery over hordes
of the old and the newly prosperous.

Libertad ¿para qué?

Extinta, ya lejana tanta lucha,
A través de un vivir tan cotidiano
Ésta es la paz: el crimen de la paz.

IV

La cotidiana vida verdadera
No miente, se denuncia.
Implacable, feroz, trascurre el tiempo,
Tiempo grave de Historia:
Los años
Que todo un pueblo sin buen norte pierde.

¿Años perdidos? Nunca.

El horizonte: brumas de la Nada.
¿A la Nada se llega?
No es accesible término.

La vida
Con su voracidad, infatigable,
Espera, dúctil, vuelve a las andadas,
Y entre ruinosos restos
Asoma el amarillo jaramago,
Que sin énfasis dice . . .

Historia.
La Historia queda abierta.
Hombres, más hombres, hombres.
Siglos como minutos. Siglos, siglos.

Freedom. For what?

Extinguished, so much struggle now distant,
through such daily living
this is peace: the crime of peace.

IV

True daily life
does not lie, it denounces.
Relentless, ruthless time goes by,
critical time of History:
the years
lost to an entire people for lack of a polestar.

Lost years? Never.

The horizon: fogs of Nothing.
It comes to Nothing?
Not an attainable end.

Life
tireless, voracious,
waits, at ease, returns to business as usual,
and among ruined remains
yellow mustard flowers appear
saying simply . . .

History.
History remains open.
Men, men, more men.
Centuries like minutes. Centuries, centuries.

FIGURACIONES

(Antes del sueño)

El magín se me ha tendido
Sobre una blanca almohada.
No aparece la blancura,
Pero siento cómo ablanda
Color tan claro el apoyo
Que se brinda a mi cansada
Cabeza.
      Un espectáculo.
Mi memoria lo prepara.
Yo soy sólo espectador,
El único de la sala.
¡Cuántas figuras del día
Sobre mi noche se lanzan
Para clavarme vislumbres
De claridad alarmada,
Tan propicia a exacerbar
Sus elementos de drama!
Y resucita mi ayer
Con la inquietud del mañana,
Ahora todo interior,
Y denso de una amenaza:
Que llegue a ocurrir de veras
Esta más y más fantástica
Representación en forma
Tan cinematografiada.

FIGMENTS

(Before falling asleep)

Fancy has placed me
on a white pillow.
The whiteness is not seen,
but I sense how a color so light
softens the support
offered to my tired
head.
     A performance
staged by my memory.
I am simply spectator,
the only one in the theater.
How many figures of the day
stampede over my night
fixing me with glances
bright with alarm,
so very apt to heighten
the dramatic elements!
Thus I recover my yesterday
with tomorrow's unease,
now everything inside,
heavy with menace:
Let it happen for real
this more and more fantastic
show in a form
so very cinematic.

A LA VISTA

Dentro de las noches sonoras,
Esas estrellas—sin sonido
Que llegue hasta el humano oído—
Participan de nuestras horas,

Lucen con fulgores discretos
Y se resuelven en figuras,
Si trémulas, nunca inseguras
A través de tantos secretos.

¿Nuestro saber nos atormenta?
Somos siempre a sentir reacios
Frente a esos enormes espacios
De la inmensidad violenta.

La inmensidad no da visiones,
Y tanto supera a la mente
Que en lo oscuro dice: detente,
Al delirio no te abandones.

Nuestro cielo visible aloja
—Muy bien nombradas, familiares—
Estrellas sobre nuestros lares,
Tan amigas por paradoja.

IN PLAIN SIGHT

Within sonorous nights,
those stars—soundless
to the human ear—
share our minutes and hours,

gleam with discreet glitters,
and are resolved into figures,
though tremulous, never equivocal
over so many secrets.

Does our knowledge distress us?
We will always feel reticent
before those vast spaces
of feverish immensity.

The immensity offers no visions,
and is so superior to the mind
that in the darkness it says: stop,
do not give in to rapture.

Our visible sky houses
—so well named, so familiar—
stars over our hearths,
by paradox, such close friends.

COMO TÚ, LECTOR

El hombre se cansa de ser cosa, la cosa que sirve sabiéndose cosa, cosa de silencio en su potencia de impulso airado. La hombría del hombre, de muchos hombres se cansa atrozmente.

Ya no pueden pararse las manos sucias por deber y recias. Muchos ojos—sin gafas—ven o entrevén más allá, aunque se inclinen hacia el suelo y sus lodazales de leyes.

Máquina junto a las máquinas o solo a la intemperie. Animal bajo un sol de selva, o en una selva urbanísima. Y los colores de la piel se cansan de su color.

Los colores se cansan de ser blancos, de ser amarillos, de ser negros: postración. Y millones de millones de fatigas llegan a formar, por fin irguiéndose, una solo figura.

Ni héroe ni monstruo. Una figura humanísima que arrolla desbaratando y arrasando a estilo de Naturaleza con furor geológico—y mental. Pero no. Es crisis de Historia.

Crisis que asombraría a los dioses mismos si atendiesen a nuestros lodos de arrabal. A los arrabales columbrarían inundados y ya arrebatados por mareas con saña de sino.

Esta vez sí se desequilibra el planeta. Sobre los magníficos se derrumban los colores, y los sujetos, uno a uno sujetos, engrosan multitudes, que son ¡ay! masas compactas.

LIKE YOU, READER

A man grows tired of being thing, a thing that serves knowing itself thing, silent thing capable of angry impulses. The manliness of man, of many men, grows dreadfully tired.

Now hands dirty and rough from drudgery cannot stop. Many eyes— naked eyes—see or half-see into the distance, even when bent toward the ground with its quagmires of laws.

Machine beside machine or alone exposed to the elements. Animal beneath a jungle sun, or in an utterly urban jungle. And the colors of the skin grow tired of their color.

Colors grow tired of being white, or yellow, or black: prostration. And millions and millions of hardships manage to form, at last, a single figure standing erect.

Neither hero nor monster. A wholly human figure that overwhelms, destroying and razing like Nature with geological—and mental— fury. But no. It is a crisis of History.

Crisis that would astound the gods themselves if they paid attention to our mud-mired slums. In the shanty towns they could glimpse people drowning and now seized by tides with fate's fury.

This time, certainly, the planet is off-balance. The colors are hurled upon the eminent, and the subjects, one by one, subjects swell the multitudes that are oh! solid masses.

Masas de hombres que podrían, uno a uno, ser hombres. Hombres como tú, lector que lees, libre, envuelto en tu señorío de piel, con un volumen en la mano, libre.

Deja de leer, mira los visillos de la ventana. No, no los mueve el aire. Responden a eso tan fugaz que fue un movimiento sísmico. Atencíon: no anuncia más que . . .

A ti también te anuncia la catástrofe de las catástrofes. ¿Terminará la esclavitud? ¿Hombres habrá que no sean cosas? Hombres como tú, lector, sentado en tu silla. Nada más.

Masses of men who, one by one, could be men. Men like you, reader, reading, free, wrapped in the sovereignty of your skin, holding a volume in your hand, free.

Stop reading, look at the curtains at the window. No, it is not the air moving them. They are responding to that so fleeting motion that was a seismic movement. Watch out: it only foretells that . . . .

To you also it foretells the catastrophe of catastrophes. Will slavery end? Will there be men who are not things? Men like you, reader, seated in your chair. Nothing more.

CITA

I

Placer por omisión: sentirse leve,
Más allá del trabajo cotidiano.
"¡Salir, salir por fin!"
Se decía a sí mismo,
Libre de aquel sudor que Adán impone.
Es grato ser de nuevo un oriente
Cualquiera
Con ímpetu gustoso hacia un transeúnte
Que nadie más percibe,
A solas por su rumbo.

Una cita da al tiempo
Reconcentrada fuerza de destino.
Era esperado. Todos los minutos
Pesaban al pasar
Con preciso rigor más implacable.

La espera nos descarga
Su futuro inminente,
Jovial, precipitado.
Corre más nuestro río: cita, cita.

Aire libre. Los ojos
Apenas atendían al tumulto.

II

Posibles poderíos insinuaba
La multitud de los escaparates.

DATE

I

Pleasure by omission: to feel buoyant,
removed from daily work.
"To go out, go out at last!"
he was saying to himself,
free of that sweat imposed by Adam.
How gratifying to be strolling along once more
like anyone else
jubilant, hurrying toward a destination
that no one else detects,
alone on his way.

A date gives time
an intensified force of destiny.
He was expected. Each minute
weighed down as it passed
with the most relentless accuracy.

Waiting thrusts upon us
its impending advent,
joyful, headlong.
Our course speeds up: a date, a date.

Outside. The eyes
hardly notice the commotion.

II

The many window displays
always hinting at possible powers.

Anuncios,
Desde el norte hasta el sur,
Por este y por oeste,
Sin cesar invadían
Con promesas—de actrices, de automóviles,
De magias—
A humanidad pulquérrima
Merced a los acosos de un jabón
Tonante como Júpiter.
¿El mundo se convierte en alarido?
Universal estruendo está copando
La inocencia del orbe.
¡Tanta prisa chirría!
La voz
Se pierde en baraúnda.
Un mozalbete con su tromba inútil
No va a ninguna parte.
Inquietud de metal
Nos escupe superflua algarabía.
Un amigo habla al otro en el murmullo
De la radio portátil.
La palabra no emerge hacia la luz.

III

. . . Y compró, también él, algún periódico.
Monotonía estúpida:
Esa amenaza de trituración
Feliz en busca del vacío, sacro,
Material de los dioses.
¿Y qué hacer entre monstruos,
A pie por una calle?

Thundering like Jupiter,
advertisements
from north to south
and east to west,
endlessly encroach
with promises—of actresses, automobiles,
charms—
on spotlessly clean humanity
thanks to the unremitting pursuit of a soap.
The world is turning into one loud shriek?
Universal racket is overwhelming
the globe's innocence.
Such screeching haste!
Voices
lost in the hubbub.
A young fellow with his useless outburst
going nowhere.
Restless metal
sprays us with debris of hullabaloo.
A friend talks to another in the muttering
of a portable radio.
No words reach the light.

III

Like others he too bought a newspaper.
Stupid monotony:
that threat of gleeful
crushing in search of the void, sacred,
essence of the gods.
But what to do among monsters,
on foot along a street?

El peatón avanza indiferente.

Colectivo vehículo.
Se aguarda en una fila, cuerpo fofo.
¡Paciencia! Se es un número,
Partícipe de forma
No, de abstracción a oscuras en la mente
De nadie.
El siglo abarrotado traza surcos
O colas
De un animal acéfalo.

Va acortándose el tiempo en el reloj
Del ya impaciente. ¿Qué hora es ya? La cita.
Mano en alto hacia un coche.
¡Veloz! Como el deseo se dispara.

IV

Abundan los deseos concurrentes,
Se arremolina el tráfico.
¿Parálisis?
       De plétora.
Tantas velocidades contradicen
Su afán.
      ¿El Globo gira o se detiene
Bajo los artilugios de los hombres?

Hombres bien amasados
En su Historia, compacta:
Presión de los más fuertes,
Voluntad de unos pocos
A caballo de muchos,

The pedestrian goes on indifferent.

A minibus.
You wait in line, body slumped.
Patience! You are a number,
not part of the substance,
but dim figment in the mind
of nobody.
The overcrowded century traces furrows
or tails
of a headless animal.

The watch shows it's getting late.
He's impatient now. What time is it? The date.
Hand high hails a taxi.
Quick! Like desire it races forward.

     IV

Competing desires abound,
the traffic moves in eddies.
Paralysis?
     A plethora.
So many speeding things work against
his urging.
     Is the Globe turning or stopping
under man's contrivances?

Men well-mixed
in their History, solid:
pressure of the strongest,
will of a few
astride many,

Dulces cabalgaduras
Como los dulces indios de montaña,
Ahora pasajeros
Por una realidad que el siglo inventa,
Ya fábula
Nunca tal vez autónoma de un sueño
¿Creador, destructor?

Mísero transeúnte.

V

El tráfico a sí mismo se destruye.
¡A pie!

Es grato apresurarse hacia la meta
Madura,
Visible en elementos
Con gracia imaginados todavía.

La ciudad, ya no selva,
O selva ya interior a un gran delirio,
Ofrecía en desorden sus tesoros,
Resonaba de anhelos,
De pasos hacia abrazos.

Entre tantos rumores,
Sus pies le conducían, transeúnte
Con dichosa premura,
Por su propio camino.

Le esperaban sus máximas verdades,
Su gloria silenciosa:

gentle beasts of burden
like the gentle mountain Indians,
now transients
through a reality that the century concocts,
already a fable
perhaps never independent of a dream:
Creator? destroyer?

Miserable pedestrian.

V

The traffic is destroying itself.
On foot!

Gratifying to hurry toward the goal
now ripe,
seen in features
already imagined with charm.

The city, no longer wilderness,
or wilderness now inside a great rapture,
offered its treasures in a jumble,
resounded with yearnings,
and steps toward embraces.

Among so much clamor
his feet led him, pedestrian
blissful with glad haste,
along his own way.

Awaiting him, his greatest verities,
his silent glory:

Amor
Que, si no mueve el sol ni las estrellas,
Blanco supremo da a la vida humana.

love,
though it may not move the sun or stars,
is the ultimate aim of human existence.

DEL TRASCURSO

Miro hacia atrás los años, lejos,
Y se me ahonda tanta perspectiva
Que del confín apenas sigue viva
La vaga imagen sobre mis espejos.

Aún vuelan, sin embargo, los vencejos
En torno de unas torres, y allá arriba
Persiste mi niñez contemplativa.
Ya son buen vino mis viñedos viejos.

Fortuna adversa o próspera no auguro.
Por ahora me ahínco en mi presente,
Y aunque sé lo que sé, mi afán no taso.

Ante los ojos, mientras, el futuro
Se me adelgaza delicademente,
Más difícil, más frágil, más escaso.

ABOUT THE PASSAGE

I look back, toward the years, far away,
and plunge so deeply into that panorama
that from the edge, barely surviving,
emerges a vague image in my mirror.

Yet swifts still fly
around certain towers, and there above
my pensive childhood endures.
My old vineyards even now give good wine.

I predict neither good nor bad fortune.
For now I delve into my present,
knowing what I know, I do not restrain my ardor.

Meanwhile, before my eyes the future
subtly grows thinner,
more difficult, more fragile, more scanty.

ESQUINA

Junto a la esquina estaba inmóvil, en tensión de espera casi ya disparada a iniciar una salida. Pasó un transeúnte, ni joven ni viejo. Ella miró y cazó su mirada, casual. Hubo diálogo más de ojos que de bocas. —No.

Ya alejado, el transeúnte iba explicándole su falta de cortesía. Caballero de idiomas: —Mi dispiace. I'm so sorry. Otra vez. Pas ce soir. Ya lo creo, muy agradable. Por aquí vengo muchas noches. Llueve . . . Oh, mi dispiace tanto.

Entró el señor en un café. —De ningún modo. Era agradable, pero tan flor del mal . . . Y esas palabras, juntas, me exasperan. Son tan insoportables como "flor del bien." No, pecado, no. ¿Infierno? Gracias, no lo uso.

La geisha: Bambú, té, versos de la dinastía XV. O la cortesana antigua de estos Mediterráneos. Quizá, no sé. A pesar de todo, esclavas siempre. Y el humillado yo también. Necesito tu libertad, tu gusto sin pecado. (X. salió a la calle, volvió la esquina.) ¡Buenas noches! No.

CORNER

She stood motionless on the corner, waiting tensely now almost primed to start out. A passerby, neither young nor old, walked past. She looked and sought his glance, casually. A dialogue ensued more of eyes than of mouths.—No.

Now at a distance, the passerby was explaining to her his lack of courtesy. Gentleman of several languages:—Mi dispiace. Lo siento. Otra vez. Pas ce soir. I agree, very pleasant. I come along here often at night. It's raining . . . Oh, mi dispiace tanto.

The gentleman enters a café.—Absolutely not. She was pleasing, but such a flower of evil . . . And those words, linked, annoy me. They are as unbearable as "flower of good." No, sin, no. Inferno? Thanks, I don't use it.

A geisha: bamboo, tea, verses from the fifteenth dynasty. Or a courtesan of ancient times from these Mediterranean parts. Perhaps, I don't know. In spite of everything, always slaves. And I humiliated also. I need you to be free, to enjoy without sin. (X. went out into the street, turned the corner.) Good evening! No.

MUY SEÑOR MÍO

Escribo para ser el blanco
De tus ojos y de tus lentes.
Pero no temas—¡oh, lector,
Ah, posible!—que yo te estreche
Con ruegos, anuncios, visitas
Y lecturas, erre que erre.
Nuestra relación—voluntaria,
Si surge—no sabe de leyes.
El que quiera picar, que pique,
Y el que no quiera, que lo deje.

MY DEAR SIR

I write to be the target
of your eyes and your lenses.
But never fear—oh reader,
ah, possible reader! that I will pressure
you with pleas, announcements, visits,
readings, on and on.
Our relationship—voluntary,
if it occurs—knows nothing of laws.
Those who wish to nibble, let them nibble,
and those who don't, let them leave it alone.

DAFNE A MEDIAS

(Un miserable náufrago)

Se aleja el Continente con bruma hacia más brumas,
Y es ya rincón y ruina, derrumbe repetido,
Rumores de cadenas chirriando entre lodos.
Adiós, adiós, Europa, te me vas de mi alma,
De mi cuerpo cansado, de mi chaqueta vieja.
El vapor se fue a pique bajo un mar implacable.
A la vez que las ratas huí de la derrota.
Entre las maravillas del pretérito ilustre
Perdéis ese futuro sin vosotros futuro,
Gentes de tanta Historia que ya se os escapa
De vuestras manos torpes, ateridas, inútiles.
Yo no quiero anularme soñando en un vacío
Que llenen las nostalgias. Ay, sálvese el que pueda
Contra el destino. Gracias, orilla salvadora
Que me acoges, me secas, me vistes y me nutres.
En hombros me levantas, nuevo mundo inocente,
Para dejarme arriba. Y si tuya es la cúspide,
Con tu gloria de estío quisiera confundirme,
Y sin pasado exánime participar del bosque,
Ser tronco y rama y flor de un laurel arraigado.
América, mi savia: ¿nunca llegaré a ser?
Apresúrame, please, esta metamorfosis.
Mis cabellos se mueven con susurros de hojas.
Mi brazo vegetal concluye en mano humana.

HALFWAY DAPHNE

(A miserable shipwreck)

In the fog the Continent moves away toward more fog,
now is a patch of ground and ruin, repeated destruction,
sounds of chains creaking through mud.
Good-bye, good-bye, Europe, you take off from my soul,
my tired body, my old jacket.
The ship sank beneath an implacable sea.
Along with the rats I fled the debacle.
Among the marvels of the illustrious past
you are losing that future, the future of intimates,
peoples of so much history that now escapes you,
slip from your clumsy, numb, useless hands.
I do not wish my self to be erased dreaming in a void
filled with nostalgia. Oh, every man for himself
against fate. Thank you, life-saving shore
that takes me in, dries me, clothes and feeds me,
bears me on shoulders, new innocent world,
to place me on high ground. And if yours is the pinnacle
with your summertime glory, I wish to entwine myself
and without a past, exhausted, become part of the wood,
be trunk and branch and flower of a firmly rooted laurel.
America, my sap: will I never more exist?
Hasten, please, this metamorphosis.
My hair moves with rustles of leaves.
My vegetal arm ends in a human hand.

LOS INTRANQUILOS

Somos los hombres intranquilos
   En sociedad.
Ganamos, gozamos, volamos.
   ¡Qué malestar!

El mañana asoma entre nubes
   De un cielo turbio
Con alas de arcángeles-átomos
   Como un anuncio.

Estamos siempre a la merced
   De una cruzada.
Por nuestras venas corre sangre
   De catarata.

Así vivimos sin saber
   Si el aire es nuestro.
Quizá muramos en la calle,
   Quizá en el lecho.

Somos entre tanto felices.
   Seven o'clock.
Todo es bar y delicia oscura.
   ¡Televisión!

THE RESTLESS

We are the restless ones
        of society.
We earn, play, rush.
        Such disquiet!

Tomorrow appears among clouds
        of a murky sky
with wings of atom-archangels
        ominous billboard.

We are always at the mercy
        of a crusade.
Pulsing through our veins blood
        of a cataract.

So we live without knowing
        if the air is ours.
Perhaps we will die in the street,
        perhaps in our beds.

Meanwhile we are happy.
        Seven o'clock.
Now the bar is everything. Delicious darkness.
        Television!

RUINAS CON MIEDO

No, no es posible recoger todos los escombros. Hay demasiados. Y así quedan entre el horror de la luz y una vida cotidiana.

La ciudad se sobrevive esforzándose frente a la quietud de las piedras, sacadas de quicio y de juicio a nivel del gran tormento humano.

Públicos esqueletos aún guardan fibrillas vivientes. ¿Volverán a volar los enviados de la Razón con sus alas de Arcángel providencial?

Y entre las formas intactas, que el azar (alguien no hombre) salvó, todavía duele a tanta resquebrajadura aquel paso de los monstruos.

Los monstruos han pasado. ¡Pasado! Se nubla el aire en que sufren las paredes multiladas. ¿Volverán los monstruos?

Hórridas ruinas sin belleza. Ruinas con el temor de no ser ni su angustia, junto al filo infernal que dispone el Arcángel.

No, it's not possible to collect all the rubble. There's too much. And so they are caught between the horror light brings and ordinary daily life.

The city survives by sheer effort before the silent stones, knocked out of kilter, half-cocked, leveled, on an even keel with the great human torment.

Skeletal structures yet retain living fibrils. The emissaries of Reason, will they fly again on their wings of providential Archangel?

And among some intact forms, saved by chance (someone not human), so many cracks still throb from the passage of the monsters.

The monsters have passed over. Passed! Around the suffering mutilated walls the air becomes cloudy. Will the monsters come back?

Horrible ruins with no beauty. Ruins with the dread of not even existing as anguish, side by side with the diabolical blade set in place by the Archangel.

BARBA CON NIDO

(Hospital de Santiago, Úbeda)

A los pies del caballo queda
Con su coraje aún, maltrecho,
Final fortuna de su rueda,
El moro español. Es un hecho
De historia. Contemplad. Santiago
Combate y remata el estrago
De aquel ejército vencido.
Pero en la barba, que no es poca,
De Santiago un ave coloca
—Paz y vida sin fin—su nido.

BEARD WITH NEST

(Hospital de Santiago, Úbeda)

At the horse's feet lies,
still enraged, maltreated,
final turn of his wheel of fortune,
the Spanish Moor. A fact
of history. Observe. Santiago
assailing and slaying the shambles
of that vanquished army.
But in his beard, not skimpy,
—peace and unending life—
a bird has built its nest.

PECAS

Mallarmé, pluma-pincel,
Compara las hojas secas
Del otoño a piel con pecas:
Tanto sol quiere a esa piel.
¡Mujer! Entre pecas él,
Si es rubia, me evoca trigo,
Que es del verano testigo.
¡Aquel blancor! Tan brillante
Que necesita delante
Sombras de dorado abrigo.

FRECKLES

Mallarmé, pen-brush,
compares the dry leaves
of autumn to skin with freckles:
Sun loves that skin so much.
Woman! When fair between the freckles
I am reminded of ripe wheat,
witness of summer.
That whiteness! So bright
it needs a shelter
of golden shadow.

ATENCIÓN A LA VIDA

–Te escucho.

–Los abetos descienden hasta la cintura de rocas, más abajo ya cubiertas de una vegetacíon verdeamarilla, algas que nos presentasen uvas de estío. En los huecos de la peña reposa el agua trasparente. Murmullo de graznidos dejan caer desde la altura cuatro aves negras. Y la mañana se encamina hacia una total vibración.

–¿Qué ocurre ahí? ¿No hay suceso?

–Todo es inmensamente suceso a través de esta calma densa hasta los bordes que sin titubear clausuran un equilibrio formidable. El agua de las olas y entre las piedras, y la piedra con sus hendiduras y tajos, y el continuo empuje con que sostienen duración y perduración ¿no están a la vista sucediendo?

–Sin embargo . . .

–Y frente a ese bosque el mar, ahora plácida lámina, que lo es reteniendo su fuerza, modulando un rumor de grises, de reverberaciones blanquecinas. Y ese barco, majestuoso como todo barco, gran máquina, pero no tan sutil como la máquina que es aquel hombre, aquel engranaje de salud, ¿no están aconteciendo?

–¿Aconteciendo? No me conmueven.

–A mí me conmueve hasta el asordado, vago, casi incorpóreo zumbido de un silencio en que, sin confundirse ni fundirse, ahora mismo se traban infinitas radiaciones conjuntas. Y todo está con todo,

"I'm listening to you."

"The firs reach down as far as the belt of rocks, lower still now covered with a yellow-green vegetation, algae which might offer us summer grapes. In the hollows of the stone transparent water sleeps. Four black birds let murmuring cries fall from the heights. And the morning takes the road toward one absolute vibration."

"What's happening there? Is nothing occurring?"

"Everything is occurring on a vast scale through this compact calm reaching all the way to the unwavering shoreline that encircles a stunning equilibrium. The water of the waves and among the rocks, the stone with its clefts and gashes, and the resolute will with which they endure, long-lasting, everlasting: are these things not occurring before our eyes?"

"Nevertheless . . ."

"And the sea facing that forest is now a placid sheet, for it is holding back its strength, modulating a murmur of grays, of whitish oscillations. And that ship, majestic like all ships, enormous machine, but not as subtle as this machine that is that man, that contrivance of health, isn't that happening?"

"Happening? It doesn't move me."

"Well, it moves me, including the muted, vague, almost bodiless humming of a silence where, without being either confused or fused, infinite radiations are being bound together at this very moment. And every-

alrededor de este hombre erguido sobre la peña, sobre tantos milenios de peña, de planta: mañana de julio marino.

–¡Verano! No me sacude el corazón.

–En efecto, nadie está ahogándose en este mar. Ningún enemigo desembarca ni ataca. Ningún menesteroso gime por ahí. No, yo no te falseo esa realidad. Los seres coinciden con su ser. Así normales, son lo que son. Como no te descubro muerte ni riesgo de muerte, por aberración eres incapaz de percibir la plena vida.

thing exists with everything else, around that man standing erect on the stone, on so many millenia of stone, of planet: July morning, seaside."

"Summer! It doesn't stir my heart."

"The fact is, nobody is drowning in this sea. No enemy is disembarking or attacking. No indigent is moaning there. No, I am not falsifying that reality to you. Beings correspond with their being. Normal like this, they are what they are. Since I do not show you death nor the danger of death, you, by an aberration, cannot perceive the fullness of life."

PENURIA

(Castilla)

Pastan rebaños de ovejas
Por los montes del invierno,
Futuro el verde más tierno,
Y hasta las ramas son viejas
En chopos de río. Tejas
Cubren adobes ahora
Sin ese matiz que dora
La tarde larga. Conduce
Todo hacia el sueño y su cruce:
Nada con noche incolora.

PENURY

(Castile)

Herds of sheep graze
over the mountains in winter,
the tenderest green yet to come.
Even the branches of the poplars
lining the riverbanks are old.
Tiles cover adobe houses
now lacking that hue that gilds
the long afternoon. Everything
leads toward sleep and its crossing:
nothingness with colorless night.

AQUELLOS VERANOS

Lentos veranos de niñez
Con monte y mar, con horas tersas,
Horas tendidas sobre playas
Entre los juegos de la arena,
Cuando el aire más ancho y libre
Nunca embebe nada que muera,
Y se ahondan los regocijos
En luz de vacación sin tregua,
El porvenir no tiene término,
La vida es lujo y va muy lenta.

THOSE SUMMERS

Slow summers of childhood
of hill and sea, with luminous hours,
hours stretched out on beaches
between games in the sand,
when the most peaceful, carefree air
never involves anything that dies,
and the festive days sink deeper
in light of vacation without respite,
the future has no limit,
life is a luxury and passes very slowly.

APENAS OTOÑO

Aparece muy poco octubre
Bajo este sol de día eterno.
Y en las alamedas son raras
Las hojas que buscan el suelo,
Donde ya barre por deber
Parsimonioso un jardinero
Mientras, paseando, estaciones
Desaparecidas recuerdo.
Ay, la memoria es quien consigue
Mi más real Otoño pleno.

BARELY AUTUMN

Slight hint of October appears
beneath this sun of endless day,
and along the poplar-shaded paths
only a few leaves seek the ground,
where a gardener, meticulous
in his duty, is already sweeping,
while I walk remembering
disappeared seasons.
Oh, it is memory that brings me
my truest, most replete Autumn.

UNA PRISIÓN

(1936)

Aquel hombre no tuvo nunca historia,
Pero tenía Historia como todos
Los hombres. Cierta crisis . . . Le apenaba
Recordar. Una vez habló, sereno.

Evoco mi prisión, no "mis prisiones."
Fue muy breve mi paso por la cárcel.
Cárcel en horas de mortal peligro.
Nos rodeaban sólo fratricidas.

"¿Hoy la suerte común será mi suerte:
Que sin forma de ley se me fusile
En nombre del Eterno, aquí tan bélico,

De sus milicias y de sus devotos?"
Confiar en mi estrella fue mi ayuda.
–¿No en Dios?–Andaba con los asesinos,

Según los asesinos y sus cómplices.

A PRISON

(1936)

That man had no history,
but he did have History like all
men. A certain crisis . . . It hurt
to remember. Once he spoke, calmly.

I recall my prison, not "my prisons."
My passage through the prison was very brief.
Jail in hours of mortal danger.
We were surrounded only by fratricides.

"Will the common fate be mine today:
that without legal formality they shoot me
in the name of the Everlasting, here so bellicose,

with his armed troops and his votaries?"
Trust in my star was my aid.
"Not in God?" "He's with the murderers,

according to the murderers and their accomplices."

AIRE EN TORNO

Admirad Nueva York desde ventanas altas:
Rodeados de espacio, lisos bloques esbeltos.
¡Oh verticalidad que a la hermosura asaltas
Con ataques de rectas! Edificios resueltos
A ser la más desnuda geometría del mundo,
Y con un solo adorno. Mirad bien: el espacio.

AIR ALL AROUND

See New York from high windows:
space surrounds smooth slim blocks.
O, you verticals attacking beauty
with an arsenal of straight lines!
Buildings aiming to be the nudest
geometry of the world, except for
a single adornment. Look: space.

ORILLA VESPERTINA

El mar en el sosiego de esta hora,
De este retiro, casi una ensenada,
Se vuelve lago, lago de crepúsculo
Donde no insisten nunca los instantes
Del apenas azul
Ya gris,
Un gris rosado que se vuelve rosa
Con indicios de malva,
Malva sobre el sosiego
Lentamente más gris, menos azul
De esta orilla marina,
O fluvial, o lacustre.

Barcas, y solitarias,
Y pocas. No las mece el oleaje.
Con indolencia de final de día
Recogen la difusa
Ya paz,
Una paz de abandono
Sobre el gris de las aguas.
Laxitud, que es ya tregua,
La dulce laxitud
Del día bien cumplido.
Con sus rosas el mar
Aspira a perfección, espera el sueño.

VESPERTINE SHORE

The sea in the calm of this hour
of this secluded place, almost cove,
evolves into lake, crepuscular lake,
where the moments of barely blue
now gray
never last.
Rosy gray becomes rose
with traces of mauve,
mauve slowly growing grayer, less blue
over the calm curve
of this marine or fluvial
or lacustrine shore.

Some boats, a few,
alone, stilled on the waves.
Lazily at day's end
they glean the scattered light
now peace,
peace of abandonment,
over the gray waters.
Lassitude now respite,
sweet lassitude
of well-finished day.
With its roses the sea
is fulfilled, settles down to dream.

VACÍO

Tu voluntad se orienta hacia el vacío.

El vacío te ahoga y lo rehuyes,
Sin cesar inminente.
Vacío
Que subraya el azul de algunas venas.
Vacío ante el oscuro
Cansancio de los párpados
Y su gran desaliento.

¿Lo sufres sin querer?
¿Eres pasiva y cómplice?

Te invade un frío pero tú lo buscas,
Y en su misma intemperie
De tarde anubarrada te acomodas,
Inventándote ya
Prematuros crepúsculos
Con su peso de tiempo, tiempo, tiempo.

El tiempo se desliza hacia más nubes,
Que se disgregan, torpes vaguedades
De nada.
Escúchame. Resiste a su atracción.

EMPTINESS

Your will tends toward emptiness.

Emptiness drowns you and you flee it,
with no sign of stopping.
Emptiness
deepening the blue of certain veins.
Emptiness before the dark
fatigue of eyelids
and immense dejection.

You endure it unwillingly?
You are a passive accomplice?

Cold assails you but you seek it,
and you adapt to stormy
overcast evenings,
concoct for yourself
premature twilights
with their weight of time, time, time.

Time slides toward more clouds
that splay out, clumsy vague shapes
of nothing.
Listen to me. Resist the allure.

VISTO Y EVOCADO

(Florencia, Wellesley)

Amarillas, cayendo van las hojas,
Una por una, cada diez segundos,
Sobre el llovido asfalto.
                    Frondas rojas
De octubres que recuerdo, ya profundos.
Alma: ¿todo lo salvas, nada arrojas?

SEEN AND REMEMBERED

(Florence, Wellesley)

Yellow leaves keep falling,
one by one, every ten seconds,
over the rain-wet pavement.
                              Red foliage
of Octobers that I remember, buried deep.
You save everything, soul, throw away nothing?

NAVIDAD EN PIAZZA NAVONA

La Navidad: un Nacimiento
Con sus figurillas de aldea,
Más aldeana si es de barro.
O sea . . .
Un dios sin forma no lo siento.
Encarnarse debe la idea.
Entiendo mejor lo que agarro.

CHRISTMAS IN PIAZZA NAVONA

Christmas: a crèche
with its little rustic figures,
more rural if made of clay,
or rather . . .
For me a god must have a form.
The idea must be embodied.
I understand better what I can grasp.

SILENCIO EN EL ORIGEN

¿Me zumban los oídos? ¿Es el rumor del mar?
¿Espacios envolventes suenan en torno nuestro?
Ocurren los murmullos como si cabalgasen
Jinetes invisibles, o un subsuelo de máquinas
A compás mantuviera faena sin fatiga.
¿El silencio produce su aparición sonora?
¿Se identifican ser y nada? ¿Todo es uno?

ORIGINAL SILENCE

Are my ears ringing? The sea murmuring?
The spaces around us chiming?
The susurrous suggests invisible
horsemen galloping or subterranean machines
working in rhythm without pause.
Silence produces its sonorous apparition?
Are being and nothingness separable? Is everything one?

SAN SEBASTIÁN

¿Quién te pone en peor estado,
San Sebastián desventurado:

El cruel que arroja su flecha
Contra un mozo que Dios acecha,

O ese pintor que como efebo
Te imagina, ya Adonis nuevo,

Y mezclando hermosura y muerte
Desea en tu martirio verte

Suave y sangriento sin un grito,
Repugnantemente exquisito?

ST. SEBASTIAN

Who puts you in worse shape,
unfortunate St. Sebastian:

the brute who sends his arrow
against a boy under God's eye,

or the painter who imagines
you as youth, a new Adonis,

and mixing beauty and death
wishes to see you in your martyrdom

submissive and bloody without a cry,
sickeningly exquisite?

ITINERARIOS

Navegar por un mar nocturno
Bajo estrellas desconocidas.

Bello amor y gran aventura.

Viajar desde la sien al pie,
Año tras año, por la amada.

Este amor es más aventura.

JOURNEYS

To sail over a nocturnal sea
beneath unknown stars.

Beautiful love and great adventure.

To travel over the beloved
head to foot, year after year.

This love is the greatest adventure.

SOSPECHA DE FOCA

(Maine)

El mar murmura grandeza.
¿Un punto negro en el agua?
Adivino la cabeza
De una foca. No la fragua
Mi magín, que nunca empieza.

Ondulación de oleaje
Sobre el dorso de una foca.
¿Encontré lo que yo traje?
A la realidad ya toca
Con su potencia el lenguaje.

SUSPICION OF SEAL

(Maine)

The sea murmuring magnificence.
A black dot in the water?
I suppose the head
of a seal. Not woven
by my fancy, never the spur.

Swells of wave after wave
roll over a seal's back.
Have I found what I brought with me?
Now language with its prowess
bumps into reality.

TAN BELLA TODAVÍA

Mudo albor. Ha nevado.
Calla la madrugada.

Hay silencio delgado
Con blancura pesada
Sobre el yacente prado,

Materia inmaculada
Frente al sol, más amado.

SO BEAUTIFUL STILL

Mute morning. Snow has fallen.
Soundless dawn.

Tenuous silence
and heavy whiteness
over the prone meadow,

spotless substance
facing the sun, loved the more.

VENECIA: FESTIVAL

La piedra más el agua más el cielo.
  Nada más. Y la piedra,
Marina y ya habitable, no se arredra:
  Aquí el milagro, helo.

VENICE: FESTIVAL

Stone plus water plus sky.
    Nothing more. And the stone,
part of the sea yet habitable, does not cede.
    Here the miracle. Behold.

AL BORDE

Olivo polvoriento del polvo de la ruta,
Tierra que se levanta de baches y relieves
Bajo el coche aclamado por un séquito espeso
De difuso planeta flotante en aire y sol,
Gris actual sobre el gris antiguo de ese olivo.

ALONG THE VERGE

Olive tree dusty from the dust of the road,
earth rising from potholes and protrusions
escorts the car along with a dense retinue
of diffused planet floating in air and sun,
new gray over the old gray of the olive tree.

CASI DEMASIADO

La nieve en el Vesubio, el sol sobre las aguas
Del mar, reverberante ya de tórrido agosto,
Naciente primavera por soleado muro,
En la esquina de sombra ventarrón invernal.
¿La gran belleza, Nápoles, puede ser excesiva?

ALMOST TOO MUCH

Snow on Vesuvius, sun over the waters
of the sea, reverberating now from torrid August,
spring beginning by a sunny wall,
on a shady corner wintry wind gusts.
Such great beauty, Naples, could it be excessive?

CUERPO A SOLAS

(Junto a la tumba de M.M.)

Caminantes: callad.
La hemosa actriz ha muerto,
Ay, de publicidad.

Entre fulgor y ruido,
Aquella desnudez
Extravió su sentido.

Era tan observada
Por los ojos de todos
Que se escondió en la nada.

Allí no habrá ya escena
Donde suene un fatal
Arrastre de cadena.

El bello cuerpo yace
Libre, por fin, a solas.
¡Uf!
    Requiescat in pace.

BODY ALONE

(Beside the tomb of M. M.)

You passing by: quiet.
The beautiful actress has been killed,
Oh, by publicity.

Between brilliance and noise,
that nudity
sent her reason astray.

So closely observed by
everyone's eyes
she took refuge in nothingness.

Now there will be no scene
where a fatal pull of the chain
is heard.

The lovely body lies
free, at last, alone.
Whew!
              Requiescat in pace.

AL MARGEN DE LUCRECIO

EL MAYOR ESCÁNDALO

Nam certa neque consilio primordia rerum
ordine se quo quaeque sagaci mente locarunt
—1, 1021–1022 y V, 419–420

¿En el principio fue la causa clara?
Frente a mí va cambiando poco a poco
La materia exquisita que se alumbra
Y se trasforma con su propio tino
como si ya supiese lo que quiere.
Movimiento lentísimo recorre
Bien previstas etapas forma a forma.
¿Cómo y por quién previstas? La simiente
Implacable, tenaz, a ciegas pasa
De su mínimo ser a sus futuras
Hermosuras: botón, capullo, rosa,
Triunfante flor perfecta con su nombre.
Yo la vi. Relaciones en su cúspide. . .
¿Es el azar quien me regala pétalos
A cada instante misteriosos? Rosa,
Incomprensible rosa irracional:
Admiro tu belleza, no la entiendo.
¿Al buen tuntún, sin luz de una conciencia
Se logran los primores, todos únicos,
De un clavel, un jazmín, una celinda,
O el grupo astral que ilustra el firmamento,
O el invisible para nuestros ojos
Que se esconde en el átomo y sus astros
Con recóndita fuerza de catástrofe?
¿Y de azar en azar, azar seguro
Siempre a tientas, feliz a trompicones,

150

MARGINAL NOTES: LUCRETIUS

THE GREATEST COMMOTION

Nam certe neque consilio primordia rerum
ordine se quo quaeque sagaci mente locarunt
    —1, 1021–1022 and V, 419–420

In the beginning was the cause clear?
The exquisite matter before me keeps changing
step by step, is born and transformed
by its own wit as if it already
knew what it wanted.
Slow slow movement goes through
well-foreseen stages form by form.
Foreseen how? by whom? The seed,
implacable, tenacious, passes blindly
from smallest essence to future
beauty: bud, bloom, rose,
triumphant blossom perfect with its name.
I saw it. Affinities within the cusp . . .
Is it chance that presents me with petals
always mysterious? Rose,
incomprehensible irrational rose:
I admire your beauty, I do not understand it.
And by happenstance, without light of consciousness,
the primal works are achieved, each one unique,
of carnation, jasmine, syringa?
And the astral bodies lighting up the firmament?
Or things invisible to our eyes,
hidden in the atom and its stars
with secret force of catastrophe?
And from chance to chance, by sure chance,
by felicitious stumblings, always groping,

Palos de ciego sobre ciego fondo,
Esa inhumana realidad —escándalo—
Ha sido y sera siempre irracional?
La vida empuja hacia más lejos, larga,
Y en un segundo rompe sus contornos,
Prolonga sus tentáculos de ensayo
A tontas si no a locas, vida estúpida
Que acierta así, maravillosamente.
¿Serás, seguro azar, tal vez divino,
Tendrás algo de un dios? Callada máscara:
¿No eres alguien, a solas energía,
Absurda por rebelde a la razón
De los hombres? Ser hombre es no entenderte,
Misterio universal. Tu luz deslumbra:
Espantosos espacios sin un centro
De intención, sin sentido, tan desnudos
Salvajes en la selva de las selvas,
Abismo abandonado al despropósito,
Y así, con tal escándalo, gran éxito.
¿Y cómo no aplaudir la gran proeza?
Razón o sinrazón propone mundo.
¿En el principio fue la causa clara?
No sé, perdido estoy, no sé, Lucrecio.
Dichoso tú, Lucrecio, que lo entiendes.

blind man's cane tapping over blind substance,
that inhuman reality—commotion—
has been and always will be beyond reason?
Life presses forward further, longer
and in one second breaks its bounds,
extends its testing tentacles helter
if not skelter, stupid life
that hits it right in such wondrous fashion.
Could you, sure chance, be perhaps divine?
Have something of a god in you? Silent mask:
are you not someone, solitary energy,
absurd for rebelling against the reason
of humankind? Being human means not grasping you,
universal mystery. Your light dazzles:
dreadful spaces with no purpose
at the core, with no meaning, such naked
savages in the jungle of jungles,
abyss abandoned to the absurd.
The result? With such commotion, great success.
How not applaud the great feat?
Reason or unreason moves the world.
In the beginning was the cause clear?
I do not know, I am lost, I do not know, Lucretius.
Lucky you, Lucretius, who understand it all.

AL MARGEN DE PO CHU-I

RÍOS DE CHINA

Este mar penetrante—campo adentro—
Es ya curso de un agua
Que esboza apuntes de esos ríos chinos
Levemente pintados, con sus brumas,
Con sus aves en vuelo, con un bote
Sin más que soledad—acompañada
Por la atención precisa de unos ojos,
Un pincel, una mano.
Con Po Chu-i diremos:
"Sólo existe una cosa
Que no me canso nunca de mirar:
El arroyo de Abril que corre sobre guijas
Y, pasadas las peñas, ya susurra."
Vayamos con Po Chu-i al río Wei:
"Ocioso allí me estoy con caña de bambú.
Desde el pretil del Wei he tendido mi anzuelo.
Sobre mi caña sopla una brisa ligera
Que mece lentamente diez palmos de sedal.
Mientras sentado espero la llegada de un pez,
El corazón errante va al país de la Nada."
Anochece. "Los ánades se duermen en parejas."
Adiós, gran Po Chu-i.
"El río acercándose al mar se amplía, se amplía,
Y la noche se alarga hacia el otoño."

MARGINAL NOTES: PO CHU-I

RIVERS OF CHINA

This sea penetrating—into the countryside—
is now a waterway
making sketches of those Chinese rivers
delicately painted, with their mists,
their birds in flight, a boat
with solitude its only cargo—accompanied
by the precise attention of a pair of eyes,
a brush, a hand.
With Po Chu-i let us say:
"There is one thing and one alone
I never tire of watching:
the spring river as it trickles over the stones
and babbles past the rocks."
Let us go with Po Chu-i to Wei River:
"Idly I come with my bamboo fishing-rod
and hang my hook by the banks of Wei stream.
A gentle wind blows on my fishing-gear
softly shaking my ten feet of line.
Though my body sits waiting for fish to come,
my heart has wandered to the Land of Nothingness."
Night falls. "The ducks sleep in pairs."
Farewell, great Po Chu-i.
"Nearing the sea the river grows broader and broader:
Approaching autumn the nights longer and longer."

See Translator's notes, p. 242.

155

AL MARGEN DE GÓNGORA

INTENSO OCTUBRE

Tenedme, aunque es otoño, ruiseñores

Se ha dorado la fronda y más aguda
Brilla en su amarillez que en sus verdores
Mientras ya poco a poco se desnuda.
Hay tiempo aún para que te enamores.

ARDENT OCTOBER

Fetch for me, although it is autumn, nightingales

The foliage has turned golden, the yellows
burning brighter than did the greens
even while baring itself little by little.
There's still time for you to fall in love.

AL MARGEN DE DONNE

MADUREZ

> *that subtle knot which makes us man*
> —"The Ecstasy"

El sumo bien se cumple: composición de opuestos.

Tranquila horizontal de la pareja.
Basta el reposo ahora indiferente
Del uno para dar a la corriente
Del deseo en el otro paz sin queja.

¿Recíproco el amor? Ha madurado.

—Y tu deseo apenas insinuante
Basta para fundirte con el mito
De Afrodita perenne que delante
De mí ya es hermosura hacia su rito.

Se logra un solo ser con doble cuerpo.

MARGINAL NOTES: DONNE

RIPENESS

> *That subtle knot which makes us man*
> —"The Ecstasy"

The whole is well completed: composition of opposites.

Calm horizontal of the pair.
The repose now indifferent of the one
suffices to give to the current of desire
in the other serenity without complaint.

Is the love reciprocal? It has grown ripe.

—And your desire, barest hint,
suffices to fuse you with the myth
of Aphrodite who before my eyes is
now beauty busy with her rites.

A single self achieved with double body.

AL MARGEN DE MALLARMÉ

AIRE DE MAR

la chair est triste, hélas, et j'ai lu tous les livres.

Ah, la carne no es triste, no leí todo libro.
Jamás se me hartarán los ojos ni las manos.
Tan enorme es la hora que yo no la calibro.
Nunca es mejor la nada que en los lamentos vanos.

MARGINAL NOTES: MALLARMÉ

SEA AIR

La chair est triste, hélas, et j'ai lu tous les livres

Oh, the flesh is not sad, nor have I read all the books.
Never will my eyes or my hands be allayed.
So vast is the hour that I do not measure it.
Never is nothingness greater than in idle laments.

AL MARGEN DE VICO

ESTE MAR MEDITERRÁNEO

ed andarono a truovar terre vacue
per gli lidi del Mediterraneo.

—La scienza nuova

I

Se esparce por lo azul una malicia
Que también claroscuro da a la euforia
De vivir en la calle. Nos gobiernan
Más que el ingenio al sol esas penumbras.

II

Late la pulsación de la marea,
Y su forma en la playa se ve incisa.
Es antigua y novísima esta brisa
Que sume en claridad mientras orea.

III

Ese mar, desde siempre navegado,
Sabe griego y latín, esboza mitos.
Natura tan humana crea dioses.
Si tus ojos bien miran, los sorprenden.

MARGINAL NOTES: VICO

THIS MEDITERRANEAN SEA

ed andarono a truovar terre vacue
per gli lidi del Mediterraneo

and they will go and find empty lands
along the Mediterranean shores
—La Scienza Nuova

I

Some malice scattered among the blue
also adding chiaroscuro to the euphoria
of living in the street. These penumbrae
govern us more than wits rule the sun.

II

The beat of the pulsing tide
leaves its shape etched on the beach.
This breeze, ancient and new,
submerges clarity as it refreshes.

III

That sea, navigated through the ages,
knows Latin and Greek, sketches myths.
Nature, so human, creates gods.
Look closely; you'll surprise them.

AL MARGEN DE BUFFON
Intendente del Jardín Del Rey

JARDÍN ZOOLÓGICO

La nature est le système des lois . . .

Rinoceronte, burdo error notorio,
Caballo, felicísima belleza.
¿Experimentos de laboratorio?
Responsable, ninguno o la maleza,
Confusión que elevada hasta su emporio
Goza de majestad: Naturaleza.

Es hipérbole torpe la girafa.
Mal se trazó el dibujo de ese cuello.
En Roma habría disgustado a Rafa-
el, che avrebbe composto il collo meglio.
Un cisne, curvo cuello, nunca estafa
Si no camina. Por un río es bello.

Tanta imaginación lo ensaya todo.
Sin escoger ofrece el resultado.
Hombre surge de arcilla blanda: lodo.
Pero el origen no se muda en hado.
¿Un "zoo" no es más que el sueño de un beodo?
Prospera y queda todo al fin salvado.

MARGINAL NOTES: BUFFON
Superintendent of the King's Garden

ZOOLOGICAL GARDEN

Nature is the system of laws . . .

Rhinocerous, clearly a crude error,
Horse, felicitous beauty.
Laboratory experiments?
No one or the tangled undergrowth responsible,
confusion carried to such an extreme
smacks of majesty: Nature.

Giraffe: clumsy hyperbole.
Poorly designed that neck.
In Rome it would have disgusted
Raphael, che avrebbe composto il collo meglio.
A swan, with its neck curve, never deceives
if it does not walk. On the river it is beautiful.

So much imagination tries everything.
Making no choices, the result is offered.
Man emerges from soft clay: mud.
But the origin does not change into fate.
Is a "zoo" nothing more than a drunk man's dream?
Everything prospers, remains, is salvaged in the end.

AL MARGEN DE SADE

EL HOMBRE COMO DEMIURGO PÉSIMO

"Escucha al relámpago, grito
Silencioso del Infinito . . ."
¿Retórica? De tempestad,
Cruel y rimbombante como el marqués de Sade.

Ay, Justina, Justina, siempre desventurada
De tanto no sufrir porque nunca eres nada,
Sólo un muñeco atroz de trapos, un pelele.
Como existir no logras, el dolor no te duele,
Ese dolor que todos quisieran infligirte.
Sin cesar irreal, viajas de sirte en sirte
Frente al ansia y la rabia de tu pobre Marqués.
Torturando está a un mundo tan débil que no es.
¿Destroza? No. Ni crea: Se le escapa la arcilla
De realidad. No sale del vacío—Bastilla
Donde sólo reside la más abstracta mente,
Que Mal y Destrucción asume idealmente.
La crueldad y el odio son fuerzas verdaderas.
Para el rival de Dios refulgen como hogueras
De su divino infierno. Mucho tienta la nada.
¿Justina destruida? Justina al fin salvada.

Veinte bombas de hidrógeno, Marqués, yo te regalo.
¿Te atreverás a ser el dios menor, el malo?

MARGINAL NOTES: SADE

MAN AS TERRIBLE DEMIURGE

"Listen to the lightning, silent
shout of the Infinite . . . ."
Rhetoric? Of the storm,
Cruel and bombastic like the Marquis de Sade.

O, Justine, Justine, always luckless
from so much not suffering because you are never anything,
mere atrocious rag doll, scarecrow.
Since you do not manage to exist, pain does not pain you,
that pain that everyone wishes to inflict on you.
Forever unreal, you go from quicksand to quicksand
in face of the anguish and rage of your poor Marquis.
He is torturing a world so weak it does not exist.
Does he destroy? No. Nor does he create. The clay
of reality escapes him, does not emerge from the void—Bastille
where only the most abstract mind dwells,
that ideally takes on Evil and Destruction.
Cruelty and hatred are true forces.
For the rival of God they blaze like bonfires
of his divine inferno. Nothingness attempts a great deal.
Justine destroyed? Justine saved at last.

I present you, Marquis, with twenty hydrogen bombs.
Do you dare to be the lesser god, the evil one?

AL MARGEN DE JOVELLANOS

DENTRO DEL CASTILLO TODAVÍA

En una madrugada
—La hora infame de la policía—
Fue el imprevisto "arresto."
Al ejemplar varón no le perdona
La mirada envidiosa—ve muy claro—
Su aplomo a tal altura. ¿Qué sucede?
Piensa. Luego delinque.

En cartuja y castillo siete años
Padece sin defensa, prisionero
Bajo la autoridad de los peores.
"¡Justicia!" Mundo sordo.
. . . Y por fin, libertad. Aclamación.
Palma rebulle, "¡ Viva Jovellanos!"
Tropas, banderas, música, gentío.

El varon ejemplar
Suscita solidarios sentimientos.
¿Guerra civil? La patria en desgarrones.
A través de los años se repite
La usurpacíon pomposa del poder.
Por el castillo vaga todavía
La sombra del egregio.

MARGINAL NOTES: JOVELLANOS

WITHIN THE CASTLE STILL

One day at dawn
—infamous hour for the police—
came the unexpected "arrest."
The envious eye—it sees very clearly—
does not pardon the exemplary man,
his poise in such a situation. What happens?
He thinks. Then he violates the law.

In charterhouse and castle seven years
he suffers defenseless, prisoner
under the most ignoble authorities.
"Justice!" Deaf world.
. . . And finally, freedom. Acclamation.
Victory begins to stir. "Long Live Jovellanos!"
Troops, flags, music, crowds.

The exemplary man
provokes feelings of solidarity.
Civil war? The country in shreds.
Over the years the haughty ursurpation
of power is repeated.
Through the castle the shade
of the illustrious man wanders still.

AL MARGEN DE LOS BROWNING

EL AMOR VALEROSO

From Casa Guidi windows I looked forth . . .
—E. B. B.

Florencia, Via Maggio tras un puente,
Puente de Santa Trinità,
Y al final de la calle Casa Guidi.
Y allí los dos poetas
Valientemente, peligrosamente
Viven y se desviven
Por convertir sus sueños en su vida
Real, la cotidiana:
Elizabeth y Robert,
El gran amor, silencio, verso, prosa,
La prosa tan difícil de los diálogos
A viva voz sin arte,
Y en la ciudad que es la ciudad soñada,
Realísima y bellísima
Con hermosura siempre verdadera.
Los años amontonan
Sus materiales brutos,
Que habrá de atravesar, y sin embustes,
La luz del corazón y de la mente.
Fugas no habrá ni vanas ilusiones.
Los amantes se afrontan día a día.
O freedom! O my Florence!

MARGINAL NOTES: THE BROWNINGS

COURAGEOUS LOVE

From Casa Guidi windows I looked forth . . .
                                    —E. B. B.

Florence, Via Maggio beyond a bridge,
bridge of Santa Trinità,
and at the end of the street Casa Guidi.
There the two poets live
valiently, daringly,
trying by all means
to turn their dreams into their real
life, the daily one:
Elizabeth and Robert,
the great love, verse, prose,
the so difficult prose of conversations
spoken aloud without guile,
and in the city, the dreamed-of city,
utterly real and utterly lovely
with a beauty always true.
The years amass
the raw materials
that the light of heart and mind
must traverse, with no trickery.
There will be no flights, no vain illusions.
Day after day the lovers face each other.
O freedom! O my Florence!

¿QUIÉN NO HA DICHO TONTERÍAS?

*Alors une faculté pitoyable se développa dans
leur esprit [de Bouvard et Pécuchet], celle de
voir la bêtise et de ne plus la tolérer.*

I

Ella dijo una tontería,
Y se escabulló avergonzada.
Mal hecho. ¿Quién pretendería
No caer jamás en bobada?
No hay boca virgen de impureza,
No hay sabio de una sola pieza.
Del infalible Dios nos guarde.
Déjame que estreche tu mano,
Con yerros hombre más hermano.
Nuestra llama en tinieblas arde.

II

Era tan inteligente
Que inventaba tonterías
Mayores que las del tonto
Sin vuelos ni altanerías,
Perdido al fin el oriente.

MARGINAL NOTES: FLAUBERT

WHO HAS NOT SAID STUPID THINGS?

Then in their minds [Bouvard's and Pécuchet's]
a pitiable faculty developed,
that of seeing stupidity and no longer tolerating it.

I

She said something stupid
and fled ashamed.
Poorly done. Who would pretend
not ever to fall into foolishness?
There is no mouth unsullied by impurity,
there is no sage entirely upright.
God protect us from the infallible.
Let me shake your hand,
a man with faults is more of a brother.
Our flame burns in the dark.

II

He was so intelligent
he invented greater
stupidities than those of the fool
without soaring or loftiness,
bearings lost in the end.

173

AL MARGEN DEL "POEMA DEL CID"

EL JUGLAR Y SU OYENTE

Sospiró mío Cid, ca mucho avíe grandes cuidados.
El niño dice: "No me leas eso."
La narración se anima. Al Cid acompañamos.
A la mañana, cuando los gallos cantarán

Juntos cabalgarán, cabalgaremos.
Comienzan las victorias. Ganado es Alcocer.
¡Dios, qué bueno es el gozo por aquesta mañana!

Con absoluta fe todos los suyos
—Entre ellos este oyente—
En el caudillo sin cesar confían.
¡Yo so Ruy Díaz, el Cid de Vivar Campeador!

Lo es, lo es. Y se despliega
Ya *su seña cabdal . . . en somo del alcázar.*

¡Alcázar de Valencia! Nada importa
que de Marruecos lleguen cincuenta mil soldados.
"¡El Cid los vencerá!" grita seguro el niño.
No hay problema, no hay dudas, no hay "suspense."
Non ayades pavor. ¿A quién le aflige?
Le crece el corazón a don Rodrigo . . .
Y a todos cuantos llega su irradiación de héroe,
Héroe puro siempre, héroe invulnerable,
Autoridad paterna con su rayo solar.

MARGINAL NOTES: "EL CID"

THE MINSTREL AND HIS LISTENER

Sospiró mío Cid, ca mucho avíe grandes cuidados.
[El Cid sighed, for he was weighted down with heavy cares]
The child says: "Don't read me that."
The story picks up. We go with El Cid.
A la mañana, cuando los gallos cantarán
[Tomorrow when the cocks crow]
Together they will gallop, gallop.
The string of victories begins: Alcocer is taken.
¡Dios, qué bueno es el gozo por aquesta mañana!
[O, the great joy they felt that morning!]
With absolute faith all his followers
—among them this listener—
placed total confidence in the leader.
¡Yo so Ruy Díaz, el Cid de Vivar Campeador!
[I am Ruy Díaz de Vivar, el Cid Campeador!]
He is, he is. And unfurled
now *su seña cabdal . . . en somo del alcázar.*
[his standard . . . on the highest point of the citadel.]
Alcázar of Valencia! No matter
if fifty thousand soldiers come from Morocco.
"El Cid will conquer them!" the child cries firmly.
There are no problems, no doubts, no "suspense."
Non ayades pavor. [Do not be afraid.] Who afflicts him?
Don Rodrigo's heart swells . . .
and his hero's radiance reaches everyone,
pure hero, invulnerable hero,
paternal authority as radiant as the sun.

175

"¡Él es quien vence a todos!" clama el niño.
Y *venció la batalla maravillosa e grant.*

"He conquers everybody," the child cries.
Y venció la batalla maravillosa e grant.
[To him was the victory, marvelous and grand.]

See Translator's notes, p. 242.

AL MARGEN DE THOREAU

CULTO DE LA AURORA

I have been as sincere a worshipper
of Aurora as the Greeks.

—Walden, II

. . .Y despertarse. ¿Dónde
Mejor que entre arboledas junto a un lago?
"Renuévate a ti mismo cada día."
Aquel hombre lo entiende,
Y la mañana es siempre edad heroica.
Una Odisea vaga por el aire
Con un vigor perenne de frescura
Frente a una flor que nunca se marchita.
Su Genio a cada uno
Le pone ante el suceso memorable:
La vida que le asalta y le realza.
"Los poetas, los héroes
Son hijos de la Aurora,"
Y en torno al pensamiento así ya elástico
—Bajo la luz del sol—
Todo el día mantiene
Trasparencia temprana.
Hombre: con firme expectación de aurora
Retornemos al mundo. ¿No es gran arte
Modificar la cualidad del día?

CULT OF AURORA

*I have been as sincere a worshipper
of Aurora as the Greeks.*
                                    —Walden, II

. . . And to wake up. Where
better than in woods next to a lake?
"Renew thyself completely every day."
That man understands;
the morning is always a heroic age.
An Odyssey is in the air
with everlasting vigor of freshness
before a flower that never fades.
His Genius places each person
before the memorable event:
the life that assaults and exalts him.
"The poets, the heroes
are sons of Aurora,"
and around the thought now so elastic
—beneath the light of the sun—
the entire day keeps
its early transparency.
Man: with certain expectation of dawn
we return to the world. Is it not great art
to affect the quality of the day.

AL MARGEN DE WHITMAN

HOJAS DE HIERBA AL VIENTO

I strike up for a new world.
— "Proto-Leaf"

Son muchos los sabios profetas
Que nos turban con profecías.
Suenen las gallardas trompetas.
¿Sabrán de los futuros días?

Enorme siglo XXI:
¿Portento será el disparate?
En las rodillas de Neptuno,
Maremágnum, el orbe late.

Imprevisible porvenir,
Compuesto de infinitos hilos.
¿A cimas habrá que subir,
Habrá que defender los silos?

Hojas de hierba nos alumbre
Luz de inagotable esperanza.
Contra la mortal pesadumbre
Nuestro corazón se abalanza.

MARGINAL NOTES: WHITMAN

LEAVES OF GRASS IN THE WIND

I strike up for a new world.
—"Proto-Leaf"

There are many wise prophets
who disturb us with prophecies.
The spirited trumpets sound.
Would they know about future days?

Vast 21st century:
Would folly be the omen?
On Neptune's knees,
pandemonium, the planet throbs.

Unforeseen future
composed of infinite threads.
Must one climb to the peak?
Must one defend the caves?

Leaves of grass light our way,
light of inexhaustible hope.
Countering the mortal sorrow
our hearts are poised to pounce.

LA INMINENCIA

. . . Entonces dije: "Sésamo." La puerta
Con suavidad solemne y clandestina
Se abrió. Yo me sentí sobrecogido,
Pero sin embarazo penetré.

Alguien me sostenía desde dentro
Del corazón. De un golpe vi una sala.
Arañas por cristal resplandecían
Sobre una fiesta aún sin personajes.

Entre espejos, tapices y pinturas
Yo estaba solo. Resplandor vacío
Se reservaba al muy predestinado.

Y me lancé a la luz y a su silencio,
Latentes de una gloria ya madura
Bajo mi firme decisión. Entonces . . .

EXPECTANCY

. . . Then I said: "Open Sesame." The door,
solemnly, secretly, smoothly, opened.
Surprised, but finding no obstacle,
I went in.

Someone within my heart was my
safeguard. Suddenly I saw a room.
Chrystal chandeliers were gleaming
over festivities still without guests.

Among mirrors, tapestries, and paintings
I was alone. Empty splendor
in reserve for a destined one.

I race toward the light and its silence,
promises of a glory now ripe
beneath my unwavering resolve. And then . . .

MARGEN VARIO

PAISAJE CON SENTIDO

Eso de Iberia es geografía.
La Península, piel de toro.
El hombre en la Historia confía.
Quiero España: voces y coro.

12 DE OCTUBRE

> *dell'affannosa grandiosità spagnola*
> —Carducci

> *España quiso demasiado*
> —Nietzsche

–Esa España que quiso demasiado
Con grandeza afanosa y tuvo y supo
Perderlo todo ¿se salvó a sí misma?
–De su grandeza queda en las memorias
Un hueco resonante de Escoriales,
De altivos Absolutos a pie firme.
–No, no. Más hay. Desbarra el plañidero.
Hubo ardor. ¿Hoy cenizas? Una brasa.
Arde bien. Arde siempre.

MARGINAL NOTES: VARIOUS POETS

MEANINGFUL LANDSCAPE

This business of Iberia is geography.
The Penisula, a bull's hide.
Man puts his trust in History.
I want Spain: chorus and cries.

TWELFTH OF OCTOBER

> *of fervid Spanish grandiosity*
> —Carducci

> *Spain wanted too much*
> —Nietzsche

"That Spain that wanted too much
with fervid grandiosity and had to and knew how to
lose it all: Did she save herself?"
"Of her greatness remains in memory
hollow echos of Escoriales,
and haughty steadfast Absolutes."
"No, no. There is more. The bemoaner is talking nonsense.
There was fervor. Now ashes? A fiery ember.
It is glowing well. It will glow forever."

AL MARGEN DE HENRY JAMES

LA MUSA RETIRADA

—The Aspern Papers

La musa retirada,
Retirada en retiro de recuerdos,
Vive reinando sola en su pasado,
Insigne entre el amor
—Tan suyo, tan secreto noche a noche—
Y las palabras de la poesía,
Pública al fin, ya célebre.

¿Fue quizás el fantasma
De un hombre que soñase
Con la belleza purificadora?
Allí está. No es ficción. No es un concepto.
En su palacio, junto al agua viva,
Es ella siempre: musa
—Con un alma en su carne—
Del verso que volando desde un nido
Asciende hasta su cúspide,
Más allá de los bosques olvidados.

Los poemas, las cartas y en su reino
La mujer para siempre ya reinante.

MARGINAL NOTES: HENRY JAMES

THE MUSE IN RETIREMENT

—The Aspern Papers

The retired muse,
retired, in retreat from recollections,
lives reigning alone over her past,
celebrated between the love
—so much hers, so secret night after night—
and the words of the poetry,
public at last, now acclaimed.

Was she perhaps the apparition
of a man who may have dreamed
of a purifying beauty?
There she is. Not fiction. Not a concept.
In her palace, beside the flowing water,
she is still herself: Muse
—with a soul in her flesh—
of the verse that flying from a nest
ascends to its zenith,
far removed from the forgotten groves.

The poems, the letters, and the woman
in her realm now reigning there forever.

AL MARGEN DE SANTAYANA

HUÉSPED DE HOTEL

*preserving my essential character of stranger
and traveller with the philosophic freedom . . .*

I

Entre desconocidos que le ignoran,
Solterón casi siempre solitario,
Vive—sin convivir—con extranjeros,
Mínimo alrededor acompañante.
Si rentista feliz, perfecto artista.

II

De incógnito caudillo de monólogo,
Pensamiento cabal, amor frustrado,
Independiente en orden, serio ambiguo,
Huésped de un astro, rumbo hacia la nada.

III

A la materia con su fe se asoma,
Y español de raíz, inglés de idioma,
Entre las soledades de su cima,
Libre de lazos, palpa el mundo lego,
Sin dioses. La verdad le da sosiego.

MARGINAL NOTES: SANTAYANA

HOTEL GUEST

*preserving my essential character of stranger
and traveler with the philosophic freedom . . .*

I

Among unknowns who ignore him,
old bachelor almost always alone,
lives beside but not with strangers,
minimum accompaniment about.
If happy pensioner, perfect artist.

II

Unrecognized master of monologue,
straight thinking, frustrated love,
independent in method, serious, enigmatic,
guest of a star, headed toward nothing.

III

With his faith he examines the substance,
Spanish his roots, English his idiom,
among his solitary peaks,
free of ties, he probes the secular world,
without gods. The truth grants him tranquillity.

ULTRAMADRIGAL

"Boca de fresa." ¿Una boca-fresa? Mirad: sí, fresa. ¡Horrible!
"Mano de nieve." Con blancura, temperatura, calidad de nieve.
¡Horrible!

¡Oh labios como labios, tan únicos: tu boca! Y esa mano, que es sólo
para seducirme su perfecta plenitud de mano. ¡Tu mano!

ULTRAMADRIGAL

"Mouth of strawberry." A strawberry-mouth? Look: yes, strawberry. Horrible. "Hand of snow." With the whiteness, temperature, quality of snow? Dreadful!

O lips like lips, so unique: your mouth! And that hand, that is only to entice me, perfect hand. Your hand!

CLERECÍA, JUGLARÍA

He recibido un cheque muy modesto.
Centavos nada más: cuarenta y nueve.
¿Limosna? Tradición sutil. ¿No es esto
El vaso de bon vino que al juglar se le debe?

MINISTRY, MINSTRELSY

I have received a very modest check.
A bit of change: forty-nine cents.
Alms? A subtle tradition. Is it not
the glass of good wine owed to the minstrel?

CARTAS

Esas cartas de amor que leen otros,
Esas cartas que, frías y desnudas,
Resistiéndose tiemblan de vergüenza
Frente a los ojos que entrevén obscenos
Los actos inocentes, los más puros,
Esas cartas raptadas, violadas
Quizá por otro amor—irresistible.

LETTERS

Those love letters that others read,
those letters, cold and bare,
that resist and tremble with shame
before the eyes that see innocent acts,
the purest ones, as obscene,
those ravished letters, violated
by another love perhaps—irresistible.

ESTO SÍ ES ABSURDO

Iba a entrar en la sala de juego, y tropezó con aquel suizo pelirrojo. "¡Dios, Dios!" Mala suerte. Y volvió dos horas después, pasado el maleficio. "Es lunes, y esta martingala no, no me fallará."

Entró en la sala de juego y vio al mozalbete del otro día. ¡Calcetines rojos! "Ese color no me va. Menos mal que hoy es lunes." Y se acercó a la mesa. "Está ganando Bárbara. Con su izquierda en la de ese tonto no pierde."

Fortuna, diosa, juega con los jugadores. Gira la ruleta, y en sus giros no acaba de revelarse el inextinguible caos, fascinador si parece un orden, cualquier orden y no descubre el íntimo vacío horrendo. Su visión mataría.

El hombre quiere ser hombre, respirar mundo. No cree en el azar ese jugador, e intenta someter la suerte a coincidencias reguladas, casi regir los azares de una bola. Nadie se resigna al total azar, al Absurdo.

He was about to enter the gaming room when he ran across that red-headed Swiss. "Oh, dear God!" Bad luck. He returned some hours later, the curse over. "It's Monday, and this betting system will not fail me, no."

He went into the gaming room and saw the same youth of the other day. Red socks! "That color does not suit me. A good thing it's Monday." So he approaches the table. "Barbara is winning. Holding the hand of that dummy with her left hand she can't lose."

Dame Fortune, goddess, plays with the players. She spins the roulette wheel, and in her spins does not end up revealing the perpetual chaos, bewitching if it seems like an order, any order, and does not expose to view the innermost horrendous void. A view of it would kill.

The man wants to be a man, breathe in the world. That player does not believe in chance, and tries to make luck bend to regulated coincidences, tries almost to rule the chances of a ball. No one is resigned to total chance, to the Absurd.

RAYO DE LUNA EN EL CIRCO

(I Fratellini)
A Ramón Gómez de la Serna

¿La luna? Querría este payaso aparecer bajo el haz amable que le proyecta un cielo de circo. Luce el fulgor, se acomoda nuestro gran artista y el rayo se le escapa, flotante más allá. Dos o tres veces se redobla aquel chasco ante la estrellada seda azul. Pero el rayo se detiene. Y precipitándose el gracioso con un martillo lo clava. ¡La luna!

CIRCUS MOONBEAM

(I Fratellini)

For Ramón Gómez de la Serna

The moon? This clown wanted to appear under the gentle beam that the circus sky projects on him. The brilliance shines, our great artist settles himself but the beam escapes him, floating out of reach. Two or three times the trick is repeated beneath the starry blue silk. Then the beam pauses. With a headlong rush the comic nails it with a hammer. The moon!

ESE JOVEN

Mírate en el espejo:
Gallardo busto.
Tienes el entrecejo
Corto y ya injusto.

Más edad te aconsejo.

THAT YOUNG MAN

Look at yourself in the mirror:
fine chest.
The space between your eyebrows
is narrow and already unjust.

My advice to you is more years.

SI EL CRÍTICO LEYESE

¿Habrá lector? Ojalá.
No me lee esa persona.
    ¡Bien está!

A su ignorancia, feliz,
Un crítico se abandona.
    ¡Gran desliz!

Dice que es mi poesía
Pura como la Madona.
    ¡Tontería!

. . . Que mi musa es de Helesponto,
Que he nacido en Barcelona.
    ¡Tonto, tonto!

IF THE CRITIC WERE TO READ

Will there be a reader? Hope so.
That person does not read me.
    All the better!

A critic has given in
to his blissful ignorance.
    Terrible lapse!

He says my poetry
is as pure as the Madonna.
    Stupidity!

. . . that my muse is from the Hellespont,
that I was born in Barcelona.
    Stupid, stupid!

MOVIMIENTO CONTINUO

Dos mariposas blancas
Volaban persiguiéndose
Con encarnizamiento
De criaturas fuertes,
Y entre ramas de arbusto
Reunían a veces
Sus frenesíes.
              Vi
Sólo un blancor moverse
. . . Y en dos se dividió.
Las alas,
          de repente
Cuatro, fueron dos rumbos
Y dos embriagueces.

PERPETUAL MOTION

Two white butterflies
chasing one another
with the ferocity
of strong creatures,
their frenzies
fused at times
among the shrubbery.
                    I saw
only a whiteness in motion.
. . . Then it split in two.
All of a sudden there are
                    four wings,
two routes,
two raptures.

DESDE EL OLVIDO

Mucho del pasado se olvida,
Y ocultándose queda quieto
Casi:
Una pulsación de secreto
En vivir actual convertida.

ABOUT FORGETTING

Much of the past is forgotten
and hidden keeps quiet
almost:
transmuted into a secret
throb of present-day life.

DESCUBRO RECORDANDO

Busqué, pedí al azar unas corolas
Entrevistas en sueños o en lecturas.

De pronto, sobre tapia solitaria . . .

Aquí están. Muy azules entre verdes,
Descubro recordando campanillas.

REMEMBERING I DISCOVER

I searched, asked at various corollas,
half-seen in dreams or readings.

Suddenly, over a solitary garden wall . . .

Here they are. Intense blue among greens,
remembering I discover bellflowers.

VIENTO DE TIERRA

Las olas desenvuelven sus bien lanzados rollos,
Y giran con avance sin cesar más rotundo
Por la curva de un ímpetu que, sin perder su pompa,
A ese final de playa tiende, se precipita
Mientras el viento opone su dirección y esparce
Las espumas: no crines de caballos ocultos,
No cabelleras tensas, o sueltas y revueltas,
Espumas, sólo espumas en el aire difusas,
Una vez y otra vez huidizas, volviéndose,
Volviéndose hacia el mar, por el viento a su mar.

LAND BREEZE

The waves unleash their well-cast breakers:
growing ever rounder they roll ceaselessly onward
along the curve of an onrush to the end of the beach,
where the intact swell spreads and races landward,
while the wind blocks its path and scatters
the spume: no manes of hidden horses,
no hair tightly drawn or loose or tangled;
spume, only spume diffused into the air,
fleeing, turning over and over, returning,
to the sea, returned by the wind to its sea.

CONSOLACIÓN

Es tan estrepitoso nuestro día,
Desgarrado por máquinas crueles,
Que el silencio recubre nuestra noche
Como si las alturas estelares
Nos consolaran de habitar la Tierra.

CONSOLATION

So noisy are our days
rent by cruel machines
but a silence covers our nights
as if the stellar heights
were consoling us for inhabiting Earth.

SALVACIÓN SOBRE EL AGUA

El silencio es en Venecia
Fundamento.
Placer de vivir arrecia,
Firme, lento.

En este "campo" sin hoja
Nunca hay pío
De pájaro que recoja
Tanto estío.

La "calle" no sufre rueda
Ni motor
Que trepidando conceda
Su furor.

Entre las casas va muda
La corriente
Del "río," que a un alma ayuda
Si la siente.

Silencio aún se edifica,
Delicado,
Sobre un agua siempre rica.
¡Tal pasado!

SALVATION OVER THE WATER

In Venice silence is
        foundation.
Pleasure of living strengthens,
        solid, slow.

In this "field" without leaf
        never a peep
of bird that might garner
        so much summer.

The "street" suffers no wheel
        or motor
that trembling admits
        its fury.

Between the houses goes the mute
        current
of the "river," balm to the soul
        that experiences it.

Silence is yet being erected,
        delicate,
over water forever rich.
        Such a past!

PALACIO

(Marina Adriática)

El mármol blanco del palacio en losas
De escalones desciende—valentía
Firme que a un oleaje desafía—
Hasta el agua y sus trazas tortuosas.

Así, palacio, porque desposas
Con elemento siempre en móvil vía
De roedor retorno y fuerza fría,
Triunfas del mar, del tiempo y de sus fosas.

Por ambición, por lujo, por capricho,
Más allá de los hábitos prudentes,
Elevas la más frágil hermosura,

Nos dices lo que nadie nos ha dicho,
Desánimo a los hombres no consientes.
La más osada voluntad perdura.

PALACE

(Adriatic Marina)

The white marble of the palace
in slabs of steps descends
—staunch courage defying tides—
down to the water and its twisting traces.

That way, palace, because you are wed
to an element always in motion
of gnawing return and cold force,
you triumph over the sea, time, and its tombs.

Out of ambition, luxury, caprice,
far removed from prudent habits,
you erect the most fragile beauty,

telling us what no one has ever told us,
that you do not accept man's discouragement.
The most daring will endures.

ANIMAL DE SELVA

. . . Y me oí mi grito de pánico
Retrocediendo ante un ataque,
Súbita protesta bestial
Que me despertó.

        Ya conozco
Mi voz más remota de selva,
La selva que arrastra por dentro,
Sonando en su noche más íntima,
Este rudo animal aún
Prehistórico.

        Le he oído
De veras gritar. Me da lástima.

JUNGLE ANIMAL

. . . I heard my cry of panic
receding in face of an attack,
a sudden bestial protest
that woke me.

         Now I know
my most remote jungle voice,
the jungle it drags about inside,
sounding in its innermost night,
this primitive animal still
prehistoric.

         I have heard
him truly cry. I pity him.

LOS CERROS DE BOGOTÁ

Las mañanas envuelven
En una bruma nórdica los Cerros
Siempre hermosos, ahora ajironados
En informes relieves esparcidos,
Monserrate y los vahos de una cumbre.
Verdores hay de frondas
Con íntimas honduras, vagos valles.

Cambia pronto la luz.
Se despejan las cimas,
Menos grandiosas ya,
Que van aproximando sus vertientes:
Descampados rojizos, casas, rutas
Donde brillan metales
Que surgen, se deslizan y se ausentan.

El panorama se divide en trozos
Múltiples, inconexos
—Tejados, chimeneas,
Suburbios de gran urbe—
Y la Naturaleza siempre al fondo
Conforta, cotidiana,
Se tiende hacia las calles, humanísima.

Es la tarde. Las cinco.
Un resplandor inmóvil
Fija una suspensión
Que se espesa, se dora, se remansa,
Ciñe bien los objetos,
Visibles dulcemente en la tranquila

THE HILLS OF BOGOTÁ

The mornings wrap
the Hills in a Nordic mist,
always beautiful, now torn
into scattered shapeless reliefs,
Montserrate and the vapors of a peak,
greens of foliage
with intimate hollows, vague valleys.

Quickly the light changes.
The peaks clear,
less grandiose now,
their slopes slowly come closer:
reddish open places, houses, roads,
where gleaming metals
appear, slip past and vanish.

The vista divides into multiple
unconnected scraps,
—roofs, chimneys,
outskirts of large city—
and Nature always in the background
constant, comforts,
reaches toward the streets, so very human.

Evening. Five o'clock.
A still splendor
fixes a suspension
that thickens, grows golden, pools,
girdling well the objects,
sweetly visible in the tranquil

Plenitud de sí mismos. ¡Temple justo!

Esa luz, tan corpórea,
Existe con aplomo sustancial,
Y por capas levísimas se extiende,
Contorno del contorno,
Superficie dorada
De toda superficie,
¿Espíritu o materia? Sol, las cinco.

Momento muy precario.
La apariencia amarilla
—De follajes, de muros, de terrazas—
Se posa embelesando, ya se va.
Preceden al poniente unos fulgores
Eléctricos.
            Nocturnos ya, no hay Cerros.
Viven focos de luz. Estrella, todo.

plenitude of themselves. Fitting mood!

That light, so corporeal,
exists with substantial aplomb,
and in the lightest of layers, extends,
outlining the outlines,
gilded surface
of every surface.
Spirit or matter? Sun, five o'clock.

A most precarious moment.
The yellow overlay
—of foliage, walls, terraces—
poses thus embellished, now is gone.
Before sunset some electric
flashes.
                Now night, there are no Hills.
Focuses of light endure. Star, all.

EL REGRESO AL LUGAR
EN QUE HE VIVIDO

El regreso al lugar en que he vivido
Tantos veranos una doble dicha
No trae pormenores de recuerdo,
Sí la emoción y el aura en torno a ella.
Ella, que ya no es ella. ¡Qué injusticia,
Y sin posible apelación a un justo,
A un tribunal! Morir así no es culpa
De nadie. Tú no estás. Y permanece
Bajo el nivel de una memoria activa,
Muy dentro de este ser que soy de veras,
El vivir que tú y yo vivimos juntos,
Actual hasta el instante en que la nada
Me lleve a mí también. Y los veranos
Seguirán sucediéndose con sombras
De consuelo, de amor, de vidas íntimas.

RETURN TO THE PLACE
WHERE I ONCE LIVED

The return to the place where I once lived
so many summers a double happiness
does not bring back detailed memories
but clearly the emotion and aura around her.
A her no longer her. How unjust,
and without any appeal to a judge
or tribunal! To die this way is no one's
fault. You do not exist. But beneath
the level of an active memory,
deep inside this person I truly am,
the life that you and I lived together will remain
real until the moment when nothingness
takes me away as well. And the summers
pass, one after the other, accompanied by shadows
of consolation, of love, of intimate lives.

TESORERO

Se presenta de pronto en la memoria
—Insomne aún—el vívido recuerdo
De aquel amor yacente bajo capas
De muchos años. ¡Eficaz imagen!
Se reanima aquel yo con el deseo
Que reanima su forma, tan ingenua.
¿Perdido ayer? Vivir atesorado.

TREASURER

Suddenly surging into the memory
—still awake—the vivid recollection
of that love lying beneath layers
of many years. Efficacious image!
That self is revived with the desire
that revives your form, so innocent.
Lost yesterday? Treasured life.

EXTINCIÓN

Cuando el amor se extingue poco a poco,
Sin choque de ruptura,
Es difícil contar las peripecias,
Conducir el relato hasta su nudo
Patético,
Detener el instante en que se pasa
Del amor al no amor
Bajo una luz de estío,
Ese estío lentísimo por cielos
Que aún iluminan con el sol ya oculto,
Y laxitud apenas perceptible
Da al tardo paso de los viandantes
Una calma de paz indiferente,
Y mientras la atención
Vaga entre brumas íntimas
Esfumándose van en el crepúsculo
Perfiles de abandonos,
Aunque infusas al alma
Queden aquellas horas tan sentidas
Por el amor, extinto.

EXTINCTION

When love is extinguished little by little,
without the jolt of a rupture,
it is difficult to recount vicissitudes,
to carry the story to its pathetic
knot,
to stop the instant when love
turns into not love
beneath a summer's light,
a slow slow summer across skies
still glowing though the sun's now hidden,
when a barely perceptible negligence
gives the late step of the strollers
a calm of neutral peace,
and while the attention
wanders among intimate fogs,
sketches of abandonment
dissolve in the dusk,
and though inspiring to the soul
those hours deeply branded
by that love remain extinct.

NATURAL O DIVINO

Pleamar. La marea se retira.
El amor se retira, ya resuelto.
Se retira la causa de las cosas.

NATURAL OR DIVINE

High tide. The tide recedes.
Once resolved, love recedes.
The reason for things recedes.

EL ADAPTADO

Después
    ¿cielo?
        No me importa.

Sino mortal no me apura.
¿Un porvenir de ectoplasma
Me ofrece tu conjetura?

Quiero vida.
        ¿Corta?
            Corta.

ADAPTABLE

And later
        heaven?
                It doesn't matter to me.

Mortal fate does not disturb me.
Your surmise offers me
an ectoplasmic future?

I want life.
        Short?
                Short.

CARTAGENA DE INDIAS

A Ramón de Zubiría,
cartagenero amigo

¡Cuánta España ha quedado por aquí,
Por estas calles y por estas plazas!

Largos balcones como corredores
Y rejas de madera
Con balaústres sobre las ventanas,
Patios profundos de otra Andalucía
Más festiva, más clara.

A nadie amenazando,
Ante el mar la ceñuda fortaleza
Que los tesoros guarda.
Y también imponente
—Obra, sí, de romanos—la muralla.

Y todo bajo sol
De trópico, luz, luz, palmeras altas,
O tempestades súbitas
De inmensidad con fábula.
Y negros, indios, blancos
Generosos de lengua castellana.

¡Cuánta vida ha dejado por aquí
La España desgarrada!

CARTAGENA OF THE INDIES

To Ramón de Zubiría, friend and
son of Cartagena [Colombia]

How much of Spain has been left around here,
along these streets and in these plazas!

Long balconies like corridors
with balustrades and wooden bars over the windows,
spacious patios of another Andalusia,
more festive, brighter.

Now a threat to nobody,
the grim fortress facing the sea
guards the treasures.
Also imposing
the wall—yes, Roman work.

And all beneath a tropical sun,
light, light, tall palms,
or sudden storms
of fabled intensity.
And generous blacks, Indians,
whites all of the Castilian tongue.

How much life around here
left by tattered Spain!

TRANSICIÓN

Transición deliciosa: castillo improvisado,
Cerradas las ventanas, resolviéndose en muro,
Muro fortalecido por tiniebla y silencio,
Silencio como parte de la tiniebla misma,
Donde ya zumban fondos monótonos, anónimos
Bajo la inmensidad inmediata a lo oscuro.
Es la dulce inmersión, despierta aún la hora,
A través de un olvido que no renuncia a nada,
Hacia el sueño cargado de porvenir creciente.
Descanso en noche astral, dormiré en universo.

TRANSITION

Blissful transition: makeshift castle,
windows closed, evolving into wall,
wall reinforced by darkness and silence,
silence as part of darkness itself,
where monotonous, anonymous depths already hum
beneath the immediate immensity in shadow.
A delicious immersion, the hour still awake,
owing to a forgetting that gives up nothing,
moving toward dream laden with growing promise.
I repose in astral night, I will sleep in the universe.

TRANSLATOR'S NOTES

p. 36: *"Potencia de Pérez"*

In Part I, stanza 1, "Crusade," with all its reverberations, was, according to Ronald Fraser (*Blood of Spain*, p 319; see full citation at end of text) used by Franco "the first week of the war while still in Morocco when he called on the army to 'have faith in the outcome of the crusade.'" Later Fraser quotes José Maria Pemán, monarchist poet who said in a broadcast over Radio Sevilla on August 15, 1936, ". . . this is a holy war, a crusade of civilization . . ."

"El Jefe" / "The Leader" was only the first of several titles given to Franco. He went on to be named Head of State, Generalissimo, Caudillo of the Party, and Chief of Government.

In Part II, stanza 1, "ORDER" refers to the proclamation issued by Franco from Tetuán, Spanish Morocco, on July 18, 1936, in which he said "At stake is the need to restore the empire of ORDER within the REPUBLIC . . . . The re-establishment of the principle of AUTHORITY, forgotten in these past years, implacably demands that punishments be exemplary and are seen to be so by the seriousness and rapidity with which they are carried out . . . ." (Fraser, p 61).

Stanza 4, the "fists reaching toward the sun," was, of course, the salute of the Republicans, also used by the Communists.

Stanza 5, "Jubilee of shirts: . . . blue summery sky-blue": the Falangist uniform was a blue shirt; the emblem, the yoke with a sheaf of red arrows.

Stanza 6, "Handsome lads smile in workshops./ Their faces to the wheat . . . the toiling girls keep on laughing." Both refer to Falangist posters of the time claiming all workers were happy under the Fascist regime. The "faces to the wheat" evokes the famous Fascist hymn "Cara al sol" ("Face to the Sun.")

The first verse of the song is as follows:

Cara al sol, con la camisa nueva
que tú bordaste en rojo ayer,
me hallará la muerte si me lleva
y no te vuelvo a ver.

[Face to the sun, wearing the new shirt
that yesterday you embroidered with red, (i.e., the red arrows)
death will find me if it takes me
and I never see you again.]

It is commonly accepted that the hymn was written by five members of Falange in a café in Madrid, La Ballena Alegre, where they used to meet. The music was by Juan Tellería (1895-1949), born in Cegama (Basque Country). During the Civil War, by decree of Franco on February 27, 1937, "Cara al sol" was declared as national hymn, the decree meaning it must be listened to with "consideration, respect, and high esteem and while standing as a tribute to the Fatherland and in memory of the glorious Spaniards fallen for it in the Crusade." The singing of the hymn always ended with the chant

España—Una! España—Grande
España—Libre! España—Arriba!

[Spain—United! Spain—Great!
Spain—Free! Spain—Arise!]

(*Diccionario de la Guerra Civil* by Manuel Rubio Cabeza, Barcelona: Editorial Planeta, 1967; p 163.)

Stanza 8, "Lie and raise your arms, / your arms or your fists"

The arm raised straight out is the Fascist salute; with the fist clenched, as said above, the Communist and Republican, salute.

Part V, stanzas refer to the constant radio broadcasts made during the Civil War by the Falangists, the only "news" available to many. The vitriolic harangues, particularly by General Gonzalo Queipo de Llano y Serra, Nationalist commander of Sevilla, made during his broadcasts over Radio Sevilla, made him famous throughout Europe, according to Hugh Thomas (*The Spanish Civil War*, New York, Harper & Row, 1961). Thomas writes: "His nightly broadcasts, full of coarse and inconsequent ribaldries, of threats to kill the families of the 'Reds' on the Republican fleet, and of boasts of the terrible sexual powers of the legionaries and the Regulares" accounted for his notoriety. In the north, General Mola spoke incessantly on Radio Navarre, Radio Castile, and Radio Saragossa, saving most of his venom for Azaña, Prime Minister of the [Republican] Popular Front Government, and on May 10, 1936, elected President of the Spanish Republic (Thomas, pp 81, 107).

Part VII, "Chorus of the Clergy" accurately describes the attitude of the great majority of the Church hierarchy and priests, almost all of whom supported

Franco wholeheartedly. Only in the Basque region did some priests refuse to go along with the all-out war (including excommunication as weapon) against the Republicans.

Part VIII. On May 19, 1938, a Nationalist Victory Parade was held in Madrid, following recognition of the Nationalist Government, that is, the Franco regime, by all the Great Powers except Russia.

According to Max Gallo (*Spain under Franco*, London: George Allen & Unwin, 1973):

"Franco . . . stood alone on a high narrow rostrum in front of a broad platform packed with dignitaries. Behind, two massive rectangular columns in Italian Fascist style bore his name, thrice repeated, and in the center, above a huge shield bearing the arms of Spain, the word *Victoria*. . . . Close behind him, but a couple of yards behind, stood the Primate Cardinal of Spain and the Grand Vizier of Morocco . . . . Flowers had been strewn on the Paseo Castellano, carnations and roses to be trampled by the soldiers. . . . Every balcony was decked with flags and splendid tapestries, or with bed linen and quilts . . . hung out under the fine rain by frightened people because a display of joy had been decreed. . . . For five solid hours, the Spanish [i. e., Nationalist] troops . . . paraded past . . . .

"The next day, May 20, was the day consecrated to the Lord. At the Church of Santa Barbara, after a Te Deum, Cardinal Goma, Primate of Spain, bestowed his blessing on the victorious general" (Gallo p 75).

Thomas, in Appendix II (pp 631-633), tries to make a rational estimate of the number of casualties from the Civil War. He believes the round figure commonly accepted of 1,000,000 lives is too high. However, a civil war is not an ordinary war, and "casualties" include not only those killed in the line of battle but those summarily executed behind the lines. Here he estimates the number of Nationalist "atrocities"—meaning, he says, any shooting outside the battlelines not to be greater than 40,000. To these categories must be added civilian deaths from air raids; the number of deaths from malnutrition, starvation, or disease directly caused by the war; deaths of political prisoners in Spanish prisons during the long years after the war ended, etc. With this calculation he believes 600,000 is nearer the mark of those who died due to the war. He does say, if one adds the number of exiles "lost" to Spain, the number could in fact reach one million.

In addition to works cited above, I consulted many other books on the Spanish Civil War. Two outstanding works, in addition to Thomas's monumental history, are *Blood of Spain: An Oral History of the Spanish Civil War* by Ronald Fraser (New York: Pantheon Books, 1979, 1986), and *The Spanish Civil War: A Cultural and Historical Reader* edited by Alun Kenwood (Providence/Oxford: Berg, 1993). Both, by using actual words and documents of the time, are invaluable, and make a strong—and painful—impact.

p. 64: *"Hotel de Ambos Mundos"*

There is a famous hotel in Havana called Hotel Ambos Mundos. According to his family, Guillén was never in Havana, but he must have been aware of the name and intrigued by it.

p. 154: Marginal Notes: Po Chu-i

Quoted lines, with one exception noted below, are from *Translations from the Chinese* by Arthur Waley (New York: Alfred A. Knopf, 1941). "There is one thing . . . " from "The Spring River;" "Idly I come . . ." from "Fishing in Wei River;" "The ducks . . ." [reference not found]; and "Nearing the sea . . ." from "On the Way to Hang-Chow: Anchored on the River At Night."

p. 174: Marginal Notes: "Poem of El Cid"

Quoted lines in Spanish are taken from *Poema de Mío Cid*, in *Romance vulgar y lenguaje moderno* (Pedro Salinas, *Revista de Occidente*, Madrid, 1934).

CITY LIGHTS PUBLICATIONS